A
HUT
at the
EDGE
of the
VILLAGE

ALSO BY JOHN MORIARTY

Dreamtime
Turtle Was Gone a Long Time, Volume I: Crossing the Kedron
Turtle Was Gone a Long Time, Volume II: Horsehead Nebula Neighing
Turtle Was Gone a Long Time, Volume III: Anaconda Canoe
Nostos, An Autobiography
Invoking Ireland
Slí na Fírinne
Night Journey to Buddh Gaia
What the Curlew Said: Nostos Continued
Serious Sounds
One Evening in Eden

A HUT at the EDGE of the VILLAGE

JOHN MORIARTY

Edited by
MARTIN SHAW

with a Foreword by
TOMMY TIERNAN

THE LILLIPUT PRESS
DUBLIN

First published 2021 by
THE LILLIPUT PRESS
62–63 Sitric Road, Arbour Hill
Dublin 7, Ireland
www.lilliputpress.ie

Copyright © The Lilliput Press and the Estate of John Moriarty
Introduction, drawings and commentary © Martin Shaw
Foreword © Tommy Tiernan

Paperback ISBN 9781843518006

All rights reserved. No part of this publication
may be reproduced in any form or by any means
without the prior permission of the publisher.

A CIP record for this publication is available
from the British Library.

10 9 8 7 6 5 4 3 2

The Lilliput Press gratefully acknowledges the financial
support of the Arts Council/An Chomhairle Ealaíon.

Set in 12 pt on 16 pt Garamond by iota (www.iota-books.ie)
Printed in Spain by GraphyCems

Contents

Foreword by Tommy Tiernan
vii

Introduction: The Trouble and Rapture of John Moriarty
xi

Horses Walking Spellbound
— *On Place* —
1

In That Divine Darkness, the Fishing Was Good
— *On Story* —
23

In That Divine Deepness, the Fishing Was Good
— *On Story* —
48

I No Longer Smelled of Thunder
— *On Ecology* —
76

The Digging Fork
— *On Eros and the Wound* —
93

Silver-Branch Beholding
— *On Hugeness* —
109

Crossing the Torrent
— *On Christianity* —
134

Hamlet to My Own Skull
— *On the Death Adventure* —
159

Genius in Every Stone
— *On Sore Amazement* —
181

Foreword

I was in a bar after a show one time and a friend of mine who'd just been to see me said, 'Have you heard of John Moriarty?'

'No,' says I.

'He's the man for you,' he said.

He refused to say too much more about it other than that John was a kind of storytelling theosopher. That was enough for me and the following morning I started digging. This was pre-Internet now so it was into a bookshop and yes they had something by him but weren't quite sure in which section. Spirituality or Biography or maybe hang on it might be in Literature. We eventually found it on the shelves marked Irish Interest. A wonder book by the name of *Dreamtime* and one look at the cover and I was hooked.

There he stood looking out, an unmannered bushman of the southern mountains. The book was full of stories. Old ones retold and reimagined. It was dead history brought back to life. Tales that for generations had had all the danger and life taken out of them by academics and folklorists were suddenly revitalized. John's philosophy of storytelling was that you don't approach them with your own agenda. You absorb the story, know it in your bones and then without deciding how you're going to tell it just open your mouth and let it come out the way *it* wants to come out. You surrender control and the story emerges differently from different people. John's wisdom, instinct and experience as well as his profound poetic sensibility meant that when the stories emerged from him they resonated with all these qualities. It was one thing to read what he'd written but another altogether to hear him tell them.

A box set of recordings was released shortly after his death, just John in front of a small group of people, talking, theorizing, storytelling and they are as important an artefact of Irish culture as you are ever likely to come across. His rhythm, sensitivities and bush brogue are enough to make you swoon. You know you are in the company of a master, an Ollamh Fodhla, a wise one. He's covered the ground that he's talking about, you can trust him.

He not only told Native American tales, Greek myths and Sufi parables but he also turned parts of his own experience into a series of what he called Irish Upanishads. They're six wisdom stories from his life that read or heard in progression offer a trail from the innocent wonder of childhood to a bliss beyond all adult knowing, encountering and traversing all the dark lands of consciousness on the way. Sounds complicated and effortful but it's not. The stories come across as stuff you might hear in a conversation with a stranger on a bus but they contain such immensities that I've been going back to them over and over for years.

It's difficult for me to follow the thread of John's writing sometimes. I don't understand some of the cultural references and I can't always keep up with the imaginative leaps that he makes but he's holding my hand when he's telling a story. He's talking to all of us when he's doing that. He had an obligation when standing in front of a crowd to make himself understood and the way John did that was the same way that all the great teachers in all the great religions did before him. He translated theory into parable.

FOREWORD

There has never been anyone like him really, in Ireland anyway. To have someone like Martin Shaw act as a guide through the safari of John's imagination is a great blessing. To listen to Martin is to hear another master speak from the bones of experience. We are lucky to have him emerging into our consciousness right now, still writing, still probing, still gifted.

Tommy Tiernan, April 2021

Introduction

The Trouble and Rapture of John Moriarty

'It might be time, if we aren't going to sicken further, to break out of our cultural grow-bag. It might be time to make contact with wild nature.'

Dreamtime, p. 172

There is a radical agency in John Moriarty's work that we don't always acknowledge.

As we behold the mighty wallop of poetical contortions and mythic philosophizing, our erudition (or lack of) may feel exposed, vulnerable. And most of us don't like that. Deep information usually arrives with dismay. So we may opt out. Easier to put the book down and go find something milder.

Because there's nothing domestic, nothing tame, nothing corralled about John Moriarty. The horses have broken from the stable.

The power of the message is that Moriarty has found a thousand ways to say something disturbing: *We have to change our lives*. And that's always radical, usually uncomfortable.

INTRODUCTION: THE TROUBLE AND RAPTURE OF JOHN MORIARTY

A Moriartian consciousness is not dependent on you living in rural Ireland, it's not dependent on you being a Christian or religious in any conventional sense. He asks of us only one thing: to move our gaze from seeing to beholding the world. He would call that Silver-Branch perception. And there the trouble begins. Because that beholding can instigate disintegration. The moneylenders flee the temple. We begin to understand the sacredness of defeat. There's a world far bigger than our temporary ambitions.

Rilke tells us it's what we secretly long for, that defeat, and Moriarty does too: that our hubris aches to kneel at immensity's door. Sometimes we may feel exhausted by his work, not fit for the task, but it actually has a kindly arm round our shoulder, urging us on. As the Sufis say, there is an angel up ahead. Life is complex, and any response worthy of the name is equally so.

This beholding tenderizes us, be-dreams us, nourishes us, challenges us. Most of all, it creates relationship. A kind of relationship that makes the hallucination of empire impossible to maintain. Thinking alongside John, we are suddenly wrestling angels, eating honey from the body of a lion, feeling the five fathoms depth of Gethsemane. He tells us that our life is our prayer mat, and we better start paying attention. Beholding is the thing – not art grants, more applause, or being born into another family or circumstance. This is *it*, this is more than enough, we start right here in the grit of our lives. He's far more pragmatic than you may expect. Many of his greatest stories take place within just a couple of hours in his life. That we commit to the luminosity of the ordinary.

This is how I would situate John: in many indigenous cultures there would come a point where the young people start to get reckless, start to push against the confines of the tribe. They would be groping for their wingspan and weren't afraid to get ugly to achieve it. This is the exact moment when they would be taken to the hut at the edge of the village. This is when they fasted in the dark wood or high mountain. In

INTRODUCTION: THE TROUBLE AND RAPTURE OF JOHN MORIARTY

short, they needed to encounter something mightier than themselves. Something wilier, more complex, exacting, demanding. Something to call forth the best in them.

Moriarty's books are a hut at the edge of the village.

Against all the possible odds, in this half-dead, burning time of ours, we have an elder worth his salt. A teacher who hasn't franchised the living spirit of his thinking, combed out the knots and watered the beer.

When you go to John's hut you will be presented with more than you can handle. *That's the point.* And in that very disorientation, some soul may enter. Moriarty's work is endlessly generous with its assumption of your own previous knowledge of myth, folklore, history. So generous it can leave us wheezing and sometimes baffled.

Stay with it. What may seem like an imposition is actually an invitation. I suggest we accept such a rare offer. This is a chance to attempt to become a proper human being. Save yourself a doctorate, and just follow his leads. You may find yourself at Jerusalem's wall. Temporary confusion can have a ritual underpinning. It's checking out if you are serious or not. The rewards are substantial.

It is deeply oral what Moriarty is doing. His themes circle around each other again and again, certain stories are invoked repeatedly, book after book. This isn't an imaginative failing: in a new age this is a very old-age way of teaching. The only strategies in which John traffics are depth and massiveness. He's isn't trotting out punditry, the books were specific in theme: Divine Ground. Both in and around us. Plotinus said the soul adores the circle, and never have I read a more circular canon. This is a magical and effective technique. Almost like Sufis whirling. As I say, we have entered the hut. We are turned from the plough to the vision pit. I wonder if whole passages are not entirely for humans anyway. So, when you find a dream, story or incident being shared a second time, or a third, there's something in it for you. I once wrote this: *Underneath a motorway there was once a road, underneath the road there was a lane, underneath the lane there was a track and underneath the track there was once an animal path. Hoof prints under the concrete.*

INTRODUCTION: THE TROUBLE AND RAPTURE OF JOHN MORIARTY

Culturally we are sickened but addicted to the zip of the motorway. We often expect our writers to be equally pithy. What we rarely expect is a man gently tracking hoof prints when all we can see is concrete. The work frequently doubles back, bellows like a stag at bay, does its strange work of disturbance and renewal.

And I want to talk about the chant. John's chant.

I was fully grown by the time I came to Moriarty, well into my second book. I knew what erudition felt like on the page, I had sat for thousands of hours in wild places, four years in a tent. Been broken open by the mysteries and left gasping. But what I had not encountered in a Western writer was the chant. The sing-song of his philosophy. The patterning of a sweat-lodge prayer in the fundament of his words, the high keen of a griever in the lintel of his images. That alone is achievement, sustained achievement. That was the *specific* key John threw to me, and I thank him right here for that. That key unlocked something. Beauty and rigour are not enemies. As a boy he wanted to be known as the 'singing lad' and I think he achieved his ambition.

So you will sense that I am proposing that John Moriarty and his work has the quality of an elder woven within its thread, that you can actually trust it. He's not invested in you mimicking his incant, rather in you finding your own. All the quests, all the night sea voyages, all the distant islands, lotus-eaters, Chapels Perilous, may be encountered within a mile of your house. Or maybe not. But a Moriartian consciousness is quite achievable in Detroit, London, Arnhem Land or Delhi.

I am presenting a small, thematic sample of John's writings. The themes range from place, love, wildness, through to ceremony and the legitimacy of sorrow. His astounding production of works in a relatively short time will more than provide a feast leading from this glimmering collection of seeds.

We offer these writings not just out of admiration, even love for the man, but out of urgency. These are not pastoral times we are living in, but prophetic. They are a moment when the world as we understand it is turned upside down. What we could think of as initiatory times. The

INTRODUCTION: THE TROUBLE AND RAPTURE OF JOHN MORIARTY

challenge is there are fewer and fewer people that can interpret such happenings in a deep, soulful way. Interpreters that don't simplify the issues, or soundbite them, starve them ragged with statistics, but ground our perception of their disclosure. I think John Moriarty can do that.

We may face a highly disturbing future. And many have forgotten that the future to the ancient world is not an idea but a goddess – the Romans name her Antevorta, her sister is called Postvorta. She is the Past. Both of them dwell within a bigger deity, Carmenta. Carmenta comes from the Latin *carmen* – spell, song, prophecy. Carmen is the root of the word charm. So to commune with the future, Antevorta, you have to charm it. Both the future and the past. And most important: you have to address both at once, because they flood into each other endlessly. That's called the Present. And it is a gift, really. If you can just bear it.

Moriarty's work has sufficient charm to attract a goddess: it faces both ways, communes with both sisters, witnesses the endless back and forth between them in the present of our own lives and times. To some that is a reckless idea, to others maybe the only thing that could save us.

Towards the end of his life, riven with chemotherapy, John threw fistfuls of his hair out his window, hoping they would commingle with the sheep wool floating about in his neighbour Tim Conner's field. A few months later that hair was the lining of a chaffinch's nest where she laid her eggs and reared her young.

Let us all have a nest with a lock or two of John's hair in it. God knows what could grow from it.

Wherever he peered, things started to emerge, take shape, become more of themselves. The Earth was grateful to have his gaze on it. John Moriarty calls the same thing from us. It's a weight, that bequeathment. Your legs should totter a little. As you will witness in his words, to live near soul is to live near aliveness, which is to live near longing and sometimes pain.

INTRODUCTION: THE TROUBLE AND RAPTURE OF JOHN MORIARTY

At least a third of this book I transcribed by hand for publication, feeling – as John's wyrd did its thing – like a Lindisfarne monk, working late. The River Dart rippled outside my cottage where Ted Hughes use to fish, and the owls heard evening readings of John's by the waters. I felt lucky. The drawings here announced themselves all at once on the last day of work.

When culture is in woeful crisis, the insights rarely come from parliament, senate, or committee, they tend to come from a hut at the edge of the village.

Let's go there.

There is tremendous, unexpected hope waiting.

Martin Shaw, April 2021

Horses Walking Spellbound
— *On Place* —

A lot of John's place he carried within himself, his psyche. But we understand that such a soul was vast, spilling out for acres around him. I doubt he'd claim its residence solely within. And the last thing he'd endorse was immunity to surroundings: 'where I am, and who I am are vastly bound up together'. But over a lifetime those locations change.

John's place is sometimes shivering in a London street having slept rough all night, waiting for the library to open with its flood of warmth and education. John's place is sometimes in a Manitoba blizzard walking with Black Elk. John's place is sometimes in Greece, adrift in swan feathers and the revels of Dionysus. There is homeless John, horny John, grieving John, no attempt at a franchised Guru-hood. John's cart of language rolled through many cultures, always bending its weight to the essence of their character, not inflicting dominion.

He urges we follow a dolphin's curve, love the crooked, adore the specific.

The scope of Moriarty's reach was not an exercise in philosophical empire-making, it was an informed, sometimes painful openness to the intelligence of the universe. There is a cost in such openness, even if there is little choice in the matter.

For now let us hear of his first axis mundi, first Holy Hills, first Temenos. Let's hear about north Kerry. Let's have him walk us across the darkness of the yard with the lantern lit, munch the hay of his thoughts, and especially bless his father's providing the money to send him to university rather than buying a farm.

Let us hear about the small magics that dart between bog and copse.

And if you come across rotten eggs in the far field, you may want to stand up and walk away.

Unless you're Jameen Kissane that is, facing down the witchiness.

Lapwings I remember. My mother lighting the lamp and in the field in front of the house lapwings calling, every call a complaint. Or so it seemed to me. And the wonder was that even when they were being battered by hailstones they didn't alter their complaints. They neither lengthened or deepened them. In all weathers, and at all hours of the night, their complaints were as elegant as their crests.

What saddened me is that they were so frightened of me. I only had to walk into the field and they instantly would become a flock of shimmerings swiftly swerving as they flew and then, as though quenching themselves, they would land farther off, among the rushes maybe, where I'd no longer be able to see them.

That's what had happened this evening, but now again at nightfall they had come back to the richer feeding grounds beside the house and that I was glad of because if ours was a house that lapwings could come close to, then surely also it was a house that angels would come close to.

Surely tonight they would come close because since darkness had begun to fall this was Christmas Eve and Madeline my oldest sister was singing 'Silent Night, Holy Night', and Chris had brought two bags of turf from the shed, and Babs had bought two buckets of water from the well, and already, its flame perfectly calm, the lamp was giving more light than the fire, with its raptures big and small.

But lamplight and firelight, that was every night,

Tonight was different.

Looking at the crib in the deep sill of our front window, I could see that the light of the highest heaven was in our house.

It was a night of wonders.

Tonight, all night, the gates of heaven would be open to us.

Riding animals higher than our horse, and wearing glittering vestments not clothes, the three Wise Men might pass through our yard tonight, and if they did our father would show us the tracks in the morning. Plain as could be, we saw them last Christmas morning.

And Santa Claus would come and he would bring us what we asked for. To Babs he would bring a blouse. To me he would bring a game of Snakes and Ladders. And to Brenda and Phyllis he would bring dolls.

And soon we would have supper with currant cake.

There was no denying it, it was wonderful, and in a glow of fellow feeling with all our animals I went out and crossed the yard to the cowstall.

Pushing open the door, I looked in and at first I just couldn't believe what I was seeing, no candles lighting the windows, no holly, no crib, no expectation of kings or of angels, no sense of miracles. What I saw was what I would see on any other night, eleven shorthorn cows, some of them standing, some of them lying down, some of them eating hay, and some of them chewing the cud, and two of them turning to look at me.

Devastated, I had to admit it was an ordinary night in the stall.

Coming back across the yard I looked at the fowl house and the piggery and the darkness, and the silence that had settled on them couldn't say it more clearly. Christmas didn't happen in the outhouses. Christmas didn't happen to the animals. The animals were left out. And since the animals were left out, so, inside me somewhere, was I.

(*Nostos*, pp. 5–7)

A HUT AT THE EDGE OF THE VILLAGE

My problem was that for my first ten years in school, I was at the back of the class. In the end, I came to see myself as my teachers saw me and as everyone in my class saw me. Without knowing it I made a compact with being last. And when, eventually, my exam results showed that I was first, I regarded it as a fraud. Nothing so trivial as a fact could give the lie to an old sense of myself.

Being last, it never occurred to me to put two and two together and conclude that Betty Guiney was fond of me. Even when she was on the bar of my bike and we were alone coming home from a dance in Listowel, and her hair was blowing back in my face, I never once leaned forward into it.

(*Nostos*, p. 18)

It suited me to be backward.

But we weren't only backward in good ways.

One day, opening a wyand of hay in the West Field, my father found four bad eggs at the heart of it. This, as it would to any neighbour for miles around, brought the cold sweat out through him. But he had to stand his ground. He had to deal with the evil, because this was piseogs, a kind of witchcraft, certainly more wicked than mere superstition.

Settling a bed of hay on the four prongs of his fork, he took the eggs, praying as he did so, and laid them on it. Then, careful that no egg would fall off, he walked towards the river. And the river, he was so glad to tell us when he came home, had taken the awful thing out of our land.

Only slightly denigrated from its Neolithic enormities, this kind of witchcraft was as common to our locality as bushes were. No year went by but some awful new story did the rounds. One story had it that a woman opened her door one morning and a skinned calf fell inwards across her threshold. Another story had it that a priest who openly confronted the evil had, within a week, to confront it, in truly sensational form, within his own church.

The evil, it was clear, was not afraid of God. It was not afraid to go into his holy house and fight him there.

That terrified us.

Among us the fabulous had become fact.

Among us the enormous had become norm.

Dimly, we were aware that this form of witchcraft was based on the belief that like creates like. The bad eggs or the bad butter or the bad meat that someone placed in a field would turn the cattle that grazed that field into its image and likeness. In other words, this didn't work by the physical transmission of physical bacteria. It worked by ritual power of sympathetic magic. Living where we did we too lived under a golden bough. Only in our case the bough was not so golden as it was at Nemi.

And so, a God who was serene and distant and uninvolved was no good to us. We needed a God who was willing to be incarnate.

Agnes Dei qui tollis peccata mundi, miserere nobis.
Agnes Dei qui tollis peccata mundi, miserere nobis.
Agnes Dei qui tollis peccata mundi, dona nobis pacem..

We needed a God, who, whatever the cost to himself, was willing to come down out of his bliss and, like the river, carry this evil out of our world. We needed a God who was willing to live on amongst us in his sacraments. We heeded the prayer Danny O' used to pray before going to bed at night, the prayer in which he invoked the protection of the four angels at the four corners of his house, the prayer in which he invoked the protection of the four Evangelists at the four corners of his bed.

One year, on the third of three Rogation Days, it fell to me to go to every field of our farm and sprinkle holy water on it. Crossing the gap into the West Field wasn't easy, but I did it.

Then one day Jameen Kissane did the terrible thing. Finding butter in the field behind his house, he brought it in and ate it.

For weeks afterwards, coming as he did every night to our house, we were afraid of him. He had eaten evil. He had eaten the witchcraft of the ages. He must be contagious. He must be avoided.

In Wales, in the old days, when someone had died, a tramp who walked the roads would be informed and, without delay, he would come to the corpse-house. Once there, he would be invited to sit at table and eat a meal specially prepared for him. Ritually, this was the sins of the dead person, and it was these sins, however mild or murderous, that the tramp was eating. Such a tramp was called the Sin-Eater.

Jameen was our Sin-Eater, but to our astonishment no harm settled on him. That should have been the end of his life beneath the golden bough, but it wasn't, not yet.

A few months later, in April, Tom Welsh and myself were coming up the road. We had cuttings Dan Scanlan had given us. Reaching the brow of Fitz's Hill we recognized a woman everyone feared coming down towards us in her ass and cart. Terrified that she would put the evil eye on us, we dropped the cuttings and to make sure we were out of harm's way we climbed through the fence where there was a break in the hawthorn hedge and went off searching for bird's nests.

By the middle of May that year we had discovered forty-six nests, and these were the nests that were difficult to find, the nests of blackbirds, thrushes, wagtails, wrens, robins, larks, wild duck, snipe, and, most difficult of all, the nests of goldfinches — three of them in the old apple trees of Paddy Aherne's orchard.

Every evening after school that's what we did. We went off to keep track of what was happening in these nests. On Saturdays, and again on Sundays, we would be out for most of the day.

Often, we would hear people saying that the countryside we lived in wasn't fit for man or beast. Mary Ann Danny O' was famous because, talking one day to a woman that had called to see her, she said, 'Isn't it a lonely place I am living in, and isn't it lonely I am myself looking out this door and seeing nothing coming towards me always but the blowin' wind and the wet rain?'

Maag Mahony, who lived in Poll, a place almost as desolate, agreed. 'Yes,' Maag said, 'there are days when I look through my door and the only thing I can say about the wind is that it is blowin' and the only thing I can say about the rain is that it is wet.'

We knew Mary Ann Danny O'. And yet, however much we tried,

we couldn't imagine her. We couldn't imagine how she lived where she did. If only someone could, it would have been a mercy to have turned her into a bush. But then, there are limits too to what a bush will put up with.

We didn't send a horse and cart for Mary Ann Danny O'.

We didn't send a horse and cart the night she came home from Danny O's funeral and slept in the bed he had been laid out in.

We didn't take her in, this woman who lived where a snipe wouldn't live.

We knew the way to her house and we blackguarded her, a rabble of us pounding her front door and then her back door with our fists, a yelling tangle of us making faces at her and screeching at her through her small, lace-curtained, cobwebbed windows.

One day, as we ran off in delighted triumph, I looked back and saw the white head of her, just the white head, craning forward in her doorway.

To this day I've seen nothing that so questions the right of the universe to exist, as it exists.

'The blowin' wind and the wet rain.'

Could it be that is an antiphon from nature's own requiem for her?

When Mary Ann Danny O' pronounced it, the word wind rhymed with mind. And maybe that was her story. Maybe the world's weather and the weather of her soul were one weather, and that being so she was able to live, into her white-headed eighties she was able to live, where a bush wouldn't live, where a snip wouldn't live.

That the universe has survived Mary Ann Danny O' leads me to believe that it could now be around for a long while.

It certainly survived long enough for Tom Walsh and myself to discover forty-six birds' nests in it.

Clearly the birds did not agree with us when we said that the place we lived in was the back of beyond. Clearly, sitting on their eggs in the hedges and in the heather, they didn't agree when we said that the place we lived in wasn't fit for man or beast.

How strange it was that we who so happily tormented Mary Ann were so tender towards nesting birds. Never once, by too sudden an approach, did we frighten a bird off her eggs. Never once, by lingering too long, did we make a hatching bird uneasy. Never once, by overforcing our way to a nest, did we leave evidence of intrusion behind us. Rather than cause the slightest upset, we were happy to walk away not knowing what we otherwise would have liked to have known. And this paid off, because, to a quite remarkable degree, it fostered an intuitive sense of surroundings in us. It was as if our oldest ancestors had whispered to us. In the stealth of our walking and, above all, in a kind of complicity with things, we were on the way to becoming good hunters.

Like good hunters, there was much that we knew.

At a glance we could distinguish a blackbird's nest from a thrush's nest. At a glance we could distinguish a linnet's egg from a yellowhammer's egg. And we knew were not to search for a snipe's nest or a wild duck's nest.

And because we couldn't seem them perhaps, few things we did gave us such silent delight as to insert a finger into a wren's nest and feel five eggs, and then, to insert it again a few days later and feel five chicks.

For want of a good terrier and a good greyhound, we didn't hunt foxes and hares and rabbits.

But that wasn't the only reason. When we were still quite young we heard a story that put us off the idea. Out in the bogs one evening, the Hard Man loosed his hound after a big, heavy looking hare. Coming to the place of carnage, he saw that the hare had been ripped open and her four babies had fallen out. On the football field and at fairs and at dances, the Hard Man was able, and made sure he was known to be able, to look after himself. He had never come second best out of a fight. But now, seeing the hare's four babies, he was troubled and instead of leaving them to the hound, he picked them up and brought them home, and by a miracle of patient kindness he found a way of feeding them and caring for them and they lived. And the Hard Man himself – well only that he didn't loose his hound at hares anymore.

That should have been the end of hunting among us.

It wasn't. Not yet.

It was unfortunate for eels that they looked as they did, that they felt as slimy in the hand as they did.

Our hunting ground was a reach of river from Paddy Aherne's to Danny Shaun's.

Apart from an acquired sense of where we would find them, under large, loose stones in the shallows, we didn't know much about eels.

To us they were a kind of shrivelled or degenerate water snake, and that gave us a right to be savage towards them.

Also there was the game of Snakes and Ladders. As far as we were concerned, it could just as well have been called the game of Eels and Ladders. And even though in school we were with uncompromising severity being taught that things were as bad as they were because of a rebellious will in human beings, we nonetheless felt that in some way or another chance was also at work. Three squares ahead on the road home a snake waited for us, six squares ahead a ladder waited for us. A throw of the dice decided whether we were engulfed into a descent or enraptured in an ascent. A third possibility is that we would for the moment go forward in safety. But that kind of life didn't appeal to us at all. And anyway, the kind of people who lived that kind of life were always complaining about us. They were always telling on us to teacher, policeman and priest. And one of them had said, you should always hit a child when you meet him because if he isn't coming from mischief he is going to it.

Ladders were for other people. But we didn't take bad throws of the dice lying down.

We took on the snake that had engulfed us. We took him on where we knew we would find him, under loose stones in the shallows of our river.

We hunted him with table forks and our glee was unconfined when we hung him aloft, gasping and wriggling, in the sunlight.

We might have been poor, someone might have put bad eggs in our hay and, following on that, all but two cows may have slung their calves, but in spite of that we were still alive, we were willing to live, and days there were when, coming home from the river, we were heroes. In that way that Michael the Archangel was a hero, we were heroes.

And now we weren't as uncomprehendingly helpless in the face of evil as we had been. We understood the thinking behind bad eggs in the hay or a skinned calf hanging from the door, Jameen had explained it to us.

There is, he said, a certain amount of bad luck in the world, and it must fall on people, not on all people, but on many people. In the way that bread and wine are the elements of the Eucharist, the bad meat and the bad eggs are the elements of a dark sacrament, a sacrament in which some people attempt to divert the bad luck that might fall on themselves onto others.

Could we in some cases, we asked him, be dealing with something more than an effort to avoid bad luck? Could we, in some case, be dealing with ill will? Is there wickedness as well as bad luck in the world? we asked him.

The only good answer to that will come to ye in prayer, he said. But in the meantime, he continued, make sure you don't persecute anyone, or anything.

That from a man who had eaten bad luck.

That from a man who had eaten witchcraft and digested it and, no harm having come to him, there he was sitting by our fire, eating the supper my mother had given to him.

In doing what he did, Jameen had liberated us.

In saying what he had just said, he had challenged me to outgrow the game of Snakes and Ladders, and something must have happened, because from that night on the eels had a better time of it.

One Sunday evening everyone but me went to Holy Hour in the church. I stayed behind to mind the house and have good fire on for Jameen when he came in.

I made tea for him and cut and buttered two slices of bread for him. Then I sat in the corner opposite him.

I was proud that he was talking to me. About how many of our cows had calved. About how much turf we had left. About what I would do when I finished in primary school.

He asked me if I felt a new power in my body.

In alarm, which I tried to hide, I said I did.

Don't be afraid of that, he said. That is natural. Grow with that and it will make a man of you.

After that I was easier in myself than I had been for the past six months or so.

More often than not now, I'd go off through the fields on my own. There were fields that I loved. Fields with a sward of natural, wild herbs. In the Hill Meadow I saw hints of Paradise. It was the only name I had for the flowers that grew there, primroses and cowslips in the dry parts of it and in the more marshy parts, buttercups and orchids.

And I wondered.

How could something so yellow as a buttercup come out of brown soil? How could something so purple as an orchid come up out of it? How could something so perfect as a cowslip come up from it?

Where did the colour and perfection come from?

And what else was down there?

What else was I walking on?

To me to inhale of a primrose was a Eucharist.

A Eucharist without suggestion of bloodshed or blood.

Sometimes I'd inhale the fragrance down to the very soles of my feet. Then I could walk the Earth without hurting it. Then I could walk in Paradise. Right here in our own Hill Meadow, I could walk in Paradise.

It was a strange world of orchids and piseogs.
It was a strange world of cowslips and bad meat.

I often thought about the priest who had preached against piseogs.

A HUT AT THE EDGE OF THE VILLAGE

On the following Saturday night, when he went into his confession box to hear and forgive the sins of his people, he sat down on thirteen rotten eggs.

(*Nostos*, pp. 8–14)

I was in the bog with my father. We were drawing out the turf. His ass would walk where mine would sink and that, while we were eating our lunch in the high heather, is what we were talking about, the lightness of step that some people have and the pure dead weight in the walk and talk of others. It was obvious to us that this has nothing to do with what we weigh on the scales. A small light man would sometimes sink to his ankles where a big, heavy looking man would leave only the faintest evidence of his passing. It had to do with mind, we concluded. Some people's mind give buoyancy to their bodies, whereas other people's minds dumbfound their bodies to such an extent they could never be *slaughánsmen*.

'Would you give me the money to go to university?' I asked my father as we gathered up the lunch things.

He was a surprised by the question as I was, because people from our background wouldn't think of going to university.

'Is that what you want?' he asked, holding his nerve.

'Yes.'

'So you don't like the teaching?'

'It isn't so much that. It's a hunger that is in me.'

'Did you ever change your mind about settling on the land? If you did we could buy a second farm. There's one going at the moment, sixty acres for seventeen hundred pounds.'

'No. That doesn't interest me.'

'So it's university is it?'

'Yes.'

'How much will it cost?'

'Three hundred pounds a year for three years, nine hundred pounds.'

'That's alright then. We'll cycle to Listowel tomorrow.'

By the time I was fourteen I had cycled the road to Listowel into a particular sense of myself. To begin with, it was the road past Jack Scanlan's, Danny Shaun's, Richie Fitz's, Con Lynch's, Jim Joy's, Willie Welsh's, Paddy Culhane's, Molly Finnucane's, Moss Keane's, Ned Spillane's. Between Spillane's and Flavin's at Dearg Owen Cross I crossed out of what we would have all thought of as our near neighbourhood, and somewhere there I would stop singing. The songs I sang had big, wide, open longings in them and that is why I sang them. I wanted the horizons of longings in those songs to lie down with the horizon of our world and make it less lonely. Singing those songs in the way I sang them, I was trying to rescue a people up into their longings. I was trying to tell them that there was something more than bog sadness to the world, I was trying to tell them there is something more to the world than the blowing wind and the wet rain. And I sang because I wanted to be heard. Passing every house, I wanted the people who were getting up in it or making tea in it to recognize me as me. I wanted them to recognize me as John, the lad who sings:

> O Molly, dear Molly, it breaks my fond heart
> To know that forever we two must part,
> But I'll think of you, Molly, and the golden sunshine
> On the banks of the Suir that flows down by Mooncoin.
>
> (*Nostos*, pp. 23–4)

Every evening at nightfall Martin Halloran would come to my house. I would hear him coming a long way off, for he would either be talking to Rover his sheepdog or he would be fighting with him. It was all out in the open, but no matter how often he was slandered in public, or worse, no matter how often he was assassinated not just in character but in his pedigree all the way back, Rover's feelings were never hurt, and not because he was thick skinned but because he instinctively knew that, coming from Martin, even the excretions were a form of affection.

It would sometimes start first thing in the morning. While Martin's back was turned, Rover would make off with his socks, maybe the last that he had, and practising his killing skills on them, would leave them in shreds outside under the fuschia hedge. Since there was big life in each of them, there was big life between them and it was as a couple fighting with each other or talking to each other that they'd come down the road, it was as a couple on precarious good terms with each other, or maybe not, that they'd come through my door.

Martin was like an old song you'd hear at a fair. Somehow, without it, it wouldn't be a fair at all, just a place where people bought things and sold things, and then went home. Whereas some people could live by the Sunday sermon, Martin must live by the song. The Christ that Martin knew had turned water to wine, and wine was for drinking, and for Martin it worked. Since he could remember, there was no tomorrow that hadn't looked after itself. But that was by no means the whole story. Martin coming into my house was Christian Piety itself coming into it. But as well as that, all of pre-Christian Ireland also came in with him. Hallowe'en came in with him. May Eve came in with him. Living on in him, the dead of Tuaim Beola graveyard came in with him.

On Hallowe'en night when he was a young man he would join seven or eight other men from his side of the bridge and they would ritually fight seven or eight men from the far side. They fought with cabbage stumps for clubs. What was at issue in this battle, Martin didn't know. I prompted him. Was it the battle between Good and Evil? He couldn't say. Was it the old, immemorial battle between Winter and Summer, the men representing Winter winning it on Hallowe'en, the men representing Summer winning it on May Eve? No. He didn't know. In the way that he looked at me I could see that the questions made no sense at all to him. Couldn't I just hear what he was saying? They fought a battle and that was that. And other men fought it. At three other borders between here and Roundstone they fought it. Wouldn't they see signs of it going to mass the next morning. All Souls' morning.

Wouldn't the road from here to Letterdyfe and beyond be white with the slush of broken cabbage stumps?

It was the same with the live coal he would bring back from the summer solstice bonfire.

'But why do you do that, Martin?'

'Didn't we always do it? Didn't we always bring a coal from the bonfire to put in our garden?'

'Was it the power of the Sun at its height that you were bringing home to your garden, Martin?'

Again, the question was outlandish and left him wondering what kind of class o' man I was at all.

(*Nostos*, pp. 511–2)

It was like that with Martin. Listening to him sometimes, I would feel that for him the wind and the rain and the rocks were newcomers. A sense I would have is that nothing can be as old as an old human being. Compared to Mary Ann Danny O, certainly as I remembered her, the stars were like last night's dew. They would come and go but she still would be there looking out at the rain, at the wet rain, through her cobwebbed window.

Like most of us most of the time, it was incidentally and indirectly that Martin revealed his sense of the world. He'd break into a story saying, I was one night in my house, out in harvest time it was, and a knocking came to my door …

That was the revelatory phrase, *a knocking came to my door*, for, given the world he lived in, Martin would never assume that it must be a human being who knocked. It could be the Angel Gabriel, it could be the Pouca, it could be the Bean Sidhe, it could be his mother's ghost, though she would hardly knock, she would just lift the latch and walk straight in, it could be Christ or it could be a changeling on her way back from half a lifetime with the Fairies.

In Martin's day little boys would be dressed like girls. The intention was to confuse the Fairies who, for some reason, most attempted to lure young boys not young girls away to their world. And yet, in a house a couple of fields away, it was a girl of eighteen years that they put their call on. But for the priest from Roundstone, who prayed all night by her Resemblance in the bed, she'd be gone to this day. He bought her back, but on his way home, he sitting wrapped up in his sidecar, his servant boy holding the reins, it was there at Inishnee Cross, a mighty stronghold of the Fairies, that he was attacked, and for three days afterwards his mouth was gone round to the side of his head.

Martin shared his word with other beings, most invisible and, whatever else, he mustn't provoke them, and in all situations, no matter how big the cost in inconvenience to himself, he must take them into account. However great his need, he wouldn't just choose the most suitable site and build a house on it. First, he would consult the invisible world and this he would do by erecting three stones at the very centre of the proposed foundation. If they were knocked in the morning, that would be that; unhesitatingly, he'd move and try again elsewhere. Never would it occur to Martin to build his house on a fairy path. Apart from anything else, there would be no sleep in such a house. All night long the Fairies would be trooping through and, given the sacrilege, it isn't blessings they'd be leaving behind.

No, Martin couldn't be a capitalist. He couldn't just look at the world and see it as an economic opportunity, that and no more.

Standing in the door one day, didn't his mother look west across the bogs to the setting Sun and didn't she see it, the shuddering, the whole world shuddering with the joy of angels, and that shuddering coming towards her and passing through her and through her house.

Opening it one night in my house, an ordnance survey map of Connemara made little sense to Martin. Mostly, it was what was isn't in it that he had an eye for. Refolding it, he handed it back to me saying, 'What chance have we when that's where we think we live.'

An awful lot that I had forgotten and an awful lot that I had yet to learn came in my door every evening with Martin.

Listening to him, I had already concluded that there was and is an

Irish Dreamtime, and so fully did he live in it and talk to me out of it that it wouldn't have surprised me if, climbing to his house one day, I saw his wet top-coat hanging from a sunbeam.

(*Nostos*, pp. 514–5)

Three days before Christmas I caught a bus to the Red Cow and from there I hitch-hiked home to north Kerry. Outside Loughhill, walking along by the Shannon, which was being carried back to Limerick by the incoming tide, a ramshackle car, a Morris Minor, drew up beside me. What I first noticed when I got in were the cold, perished hands at the wheel. Hands become stiff and awkward in their joints. Even as I talked to him, inevitably about the bad weather, my eyes kept coming back to them. Looking at them, an Elizabethan would say that they were the hands of a man of eighty winters, because a man of eighty winters is much older than a man of eighty years. A winter endured is wind endured and it is rain endured. It is a house whining at every sash, upstairs and downstairs, endured. For nights on end endured. Winter means a low, watery Sun that doesn't come round, not once in three months, to the north gable of the house. A week of gales shaking its lichens off an old apple tree followed by a week of wind and rain, that would leave you having pity for bushes, that in itself would put ten years on a man's life.

There could be no doubt about it. I was sitting with a man of eighty south-western winters. And it showed. In the creak, as of a creaking door, that his voice had become, it showed. It showed in the missing shirt buttons, leaving his chest as perished looking as his hands, a place of wispy whisperings whenever we turned a bend into the wind.

An old bachelor farmer if ever there was one, he was down now he told me, to nine cows. 'How, with your hands as they are, do you milk nine cows?' I asked him.

'Whatever life is in me I get from the paps of cows,' he creaked. 'And do you know the grandest thing in the world? The grandest thing in the world is when you are teaching a calf to drink milk from a bucket. You must know what it is like yourself. You're Mororty [sic], aren't you? I'd know you anywhere I met you from your mother. Ye had cows, so you must know what I'm talking about when you put your first two fingers into a calf's mouth and he curls his tongue round them, holding them tight against the ridged roof behind his moist nostrils and sucking them, drawing on them, like they were one of his mother's paps. That's when the life of the world comes into you, comes out into you from somewhere inside you, you drawing his mouth down into the milk, sinking your hand in it, so that he gets a taste of it. Three or four days later and he'll need no pap, but then another cow or maybe two cows will be calving and I'll tell you what you know yourself, being Mary O'Brien's son, a calf's tongue curled round a piece of old leather like me turns it back into shorthorn hide, its fur licked into waves.'

He left me off in Tarbert and as I walked up the road, climbing the hill towards Tarmons, the Shannon a grandeur of water behind me, it occurred to me that an English sentence correctly translated into ancient Greek was what made the difference, separating my life from his life, separating my life from the life of my father and mother, she telling Gret Welsh that, what with my drainpipe trousers and long hair, I didn't even look like a fact of life.

But a calf's tongue curled around my first two fingers and therefore curled round a core of my being keeping its animal life alive in it – that indeed was a fact of life that I well remembered, and that was restored to me now, coming up to Christmas, by a man of eighty winters who, when he shook my hand with his perished hand, left the waves of licked cow's fur in it.

Coming to the top of Tarmons Hill I felt, as I so often did before, that I had come to a divide. Geographers talk of a physical, continental divide in North America. Mostly, it runs down along the spine of the Rocky Mountains. On one side of this divides the rivers flow west into the Pacific. On the other side of it they flow east and then north to the

Arctic Ocean or south to the Gulf of Mexico. For me, Tarmons was a spiritual divide. Behind me, the Shannon flowing through it, was a landscape that had in it a remembrance of Paradise. Ahead of me, the little tributaries of the Gayle flowing through it, was a landscape that had in it no very evident reminders of Paradise.

These are wuthering places, I thought. Places in which people and bushes and cattle are weathered, are wuthered, and this is one of them. All these fields, I could see, had been reclaimed or claimed for the first time from beneath the great raised bogs, only islands of which now remained. And a sense I had is that this land, rushy and wet, didn't want to be claimed, didn't want to be coerced into human intention and purpose. It was as though it resented its rebirth or its abortion back into daylight. And the best thing therefore to do with it would be to say a requiem mass on it, for it, and then, letting nature have its way with it, let a new raised bog over grow it. As bog, with patches of bog myrtle, bog cotton and bog asphodel – as bog, with patches of sphagnum moss red and green – as bog, with patches of heather and sedge and dwarf gorse in it – as bog, with wild duck and curlew and snipe nesting in it and calling in in it – as bog, this place I was born in and grew up in would remember Paradise, and it would give us images and metaphors for how we felt when we are in love. And then instead of me having to go and live next door to Lucy by Derwent Water I could ask Lucy to come and live next door to me. I could ask Lycidas to come, and in the lovely month of May there wouldn't be a snipe's nest or a curlew's nest or a wild duck's nest that we wouldn't know, and that way it would be about us and our place that Theocritus and Virgil and Tasso and Spenser and Sidney and Milton and Wordsworth would be singing.

But no. This wasn't Sicily in the Golden Age, and Amaryllis didn't live here, nor did Damoetas live here. This was where I grew up and Paddy Culhane lived here, and Mary Anne Danny O' lived here, and it was Mary Anne Danny O's eclogue that gave its own distinctive voice to the place:

> Isn't it a lonely place I am living in, and isn't it lonely I am myself looking out this door and seeing nothing coming towards me always but the blowin' wind and the wet rain.

Maag Mahony who lived in Poll agreed. Yes, Maag said, there are days when I look through my door too and the only thing I can say about the wind is that it is blowing and the only thing I can say about the rain is that it is wet.

North Kerry eclogues.

North Kerry antiphons.

A world, and it a wuthering world, coming to consciousness of itself.

And yet, Mary Anne Danny O' was in all ways a more tremendous woman, a more tremendous being, a more tremendous Zoa, than Amaryllis would ever be. And she lived in a more tremendous world than Amaryllis lived in.

Of one thing I was sure. Neither Theocritus nor Milton had the measure, the literary measure, of Mary Ann Danny O', nor had either of them the measure of Poll, the few green fields aborted from the bog where Maag Mahony milked her cows, fed her hens and her horse, harnessed her ass and tackled him to her cart at around six o'clock, every morning, winter and summer, and then set out for the Creamery in Moyvane.

It occurred to me, walking a stretch of it now, that the road from Tarmons to Poll ran deeper into the world than the road from Athens to the Labyrinth did. Myths that walked with me on the road to the Labyrinth wouldn't, because they couldn't, walk with me on the road to Poll. I'd be altogether better able to sit in her house with Pasiphae than I would to sit in her house with Maag.

Myth had encompassed Pasiphae, it hadn't encompassed Maag.

Myth had imagined Pasiphae to herself, it hadn't imagined Maag to herself.

Somewhere on the road to Poll, myth reached its limit and turned back on itself.

Somewhere on the road to Poll, Western literature reached its limit and turned back on itself.

Somewhere on the road to Poll, the thread that Ariadne gave to our Western hero ran out and the golden bough no longer lighted his way.

Somewhere on the road to Poll, Jesus walked forward alone beyond those limits of daring reached but not overpassed by Herakles, Perseus and Theseus.

Whether Jesus made it all the way to Poll we do not know. What we do know is that on the road to Poll a saviour will soon find out what he is made of.

(*Nostos*, pp. 147–50)

If it is Upanishads and Gitas we are looking for we needn't leave home.

I remembered a story Martin Halloran told me. It is a story about a man called Feshtus O'Malley from Oorid in Connemara. One night Feshtus dreamed that there was a great hoard of treasure buried beside O'Brien's Bridge in Limerick. Off Feshtus went the next day and three days later he was there. All morning he walked up and down and in and out and back and forth, looking all the time for the treasure. A cobbler working in his house near the bridge saw the goings-on of Feshtus. In the end he came out and greeted him and asked him was it how he had lost something. No, Feshtus said, but 'tis how I dreamed four nights ago that great treasure is buried here. 'And what's your name?' the cobbler asked. 'My name is Feshtus O'Malley.' 'And you're from where?' 'From a place called Oorid in Connemara.' 'That's awful strange,' the cobbler said, 'because didn't I dream myself last night about you and your house, and what the dream told me was that under a flagstone inside your door there is more treasure than the Vikings, for all their raiding, ever laid their hungry hands on.' In less than three days Feshtus was home and sure enough there it was. All his life long, walking in and out through his own door he had been walking on top of it.

And there's the story of the man who despaired of the West. Going to the East he lived in a Zen monastery for years. In the airport, coming home, his teacher, who was a great master, gave him a present. In the plane waiting for take-off, the young man unwrapped the gift and to his great surprise and annoyance it was a copy, very beautifully bound, of the Bible.

The master telling him, find it in your own tradition.

The master telling him, walk your own songline.

The master telling him, you don't need to go to O'Brien's Bridge. It is under the flagstone inside your own door.

Since it is the mystical journey we are talking about it isn't of course as simple as lifting a flagstone. Under the flagstone might be a labyrinth or under it might be a very great treasure indeed, the writings of the Christian mystics, among them *The Dark Night of the Soul* and *The Ascent of Mount Carmel* by St John of the Cross. Reading these latter at random most people will soon know whether to drop the flagstone back down on top of them or to continue the quest.

(*Turtle, Vol. 3*, p. 179)

In That Divine Darkness, the Fishing Was Good

— *On Story* —

Everyone is asking for a story, a new story, a big story. As if the wayward choreography of our life counts for nothing. As if we didn't have the red mud of myth on our hooves to begin with. In the first of two selections dedicated to John's handling of story, we begin with stories grounded in localized experience. It's only by trading a little growth do we gain some depth. Moriarty has the storyteller's gift of playing the tale like a concertina – he stretches out its massiveness – and poignancy drops like rain around us. In the story of Big Mike, we have a man taking his seemingly doomed boat out into the waters, night after night. What terrifies his friends is that he seems to be carrying no nets.

In the medieval telling of Parzival, *the only place the wounded Grail king finds relief from his wound is by fishing in the deep lake. He is not – as later versions insist – waiting for his momentary reprieve every Good Friday. It is by soulful descent rather than heavenly blessing that he receives some relief from his agonies. And there fishes Big Mike, and all of us. In that divine darkness, in that divine deepness, John tells us, from the very crucible of his truthfulness, that the fishing is, indeed, good. John warns us that it's not darkness that separates us from the rest of creation; it is the accelerated, strip-lit brightness of a buzzed up modern mind. He advocates tallow wick and lantern, and plenty of room for shadow to even begin to see more clearly.*

These seemingly humble stories are serious gold in the pocket, and it is an example of Moriarty's subtlety that he presents them as such. He is constantly rescuing tiny scraps from the wastepaper basket. He returns them to their rightful stature, and the implicit invitation is that we may start to brood on the circumstance of our own life with a similar care and patience.

In John's world, the Big Story arrives every day.

Big Mike he was called and ever since he came home to the island, after thirty years at sea, people felt there something inwardly torn or broken about him. He's had a rough crossing somewhere.

By nightfall, on the day of his arrival, everyone knew he was back. Everyone who saw it was glad to see smoke from the old chimney.

After a couple of days anyone who hadn't seen him looked forward to meeting him on Sunday after mass. He didn't show up. Neither was there sight or light of him the following Sunday. One thing, and that a big thing, they knew about him now: he wasn't rowing in behind Christ.

Sarah Coyne didn't like it. Not that Sarah was pious. As midwife on the island, Sarah had helped to bring him into the world and if only for the sake of his dead father and his dead mother, she wanted to hear that he'd fared fairly well in the world.

One night, her curiosity getting the better other, she went up to see him.

'Jesus, Mary and Joseph!' she said to Jim Barlow an hour or so later in her own house, 'Jesus, Mary and Joseph! He has and yet he hasn't come back. He is still out there somewhere in the roaring forties of the sea, or in the roaring forties of his mind, out where the sound of the last foghorn and the life of the last lighthouse cannot reach him.'

Trying to throw a lifeline to him she was the next day when she sent him up a loaf of homemade brown bread and a jar of gooseberry jam neatly labelled and dated.

'Look at the brains of sheep and fish,' Marcus King said to Sarah one day. 'You've seen them, haven't you? You've seen how furled they are. That's what's what happened to him, Sarah. He unfurled too much of his mind to the wind. He let out too much sail to the wind.' No, Sarah, no. We aren't keeled for those waters. We aren't keeled for the waters Big Mike was blown into.

Walking home from mass that Sunday with Sarah, Marcus was a strong, able man. Little did he or she suspect that within a year he'd be passing these same house, Lavelle's house, Burke's house, Coyne's house, his own house, in a coffin.

On the night after the funeral, lying awake in bed, Ned Lavelle was wondering who now would man the beam oars in his eight-oar curragh.

Big Mike was the only prospect.

One day, making a breast of it, he asked him.

That evening there was the sound of other footsteps, footsteps the women hadn't heard before, on the gravel path going down to the sea.

Coming to their doors they wished him well. Something in him evoked a need in them. The need Sarah Coyne had felt when she sent him up the loaf of homemade brown bread and the pot of gooseberry jam.

As was their custom, they waited to watch the curraghs going out, seventeen of them, out wide around the breakers, out around the headland, into the ocean.

Next morning at daybreak they would, once again, be standing in their doors, counting them, more anxiously this time, as they came into view around the headland.

That was the pattern of island life, the sound of footsteps; in ones and twos and threes, going down to the sea every evening, coming back every morning.

Within a year Big Mike had fallen in with all the old ways of his people. Outwardly, there was nothing odd or different about him. He even showed up at mass a few times. And yet he was strange.

Sometimes in May, hauling their pots, fishermen in these waters would find a pale, delicately blue lobster. He, they would tell you, was a stray. He had come from the limestone seafloors to the south. Down there his colouring camouflaged him. Up here, on a seafloor of granite and schist, he stood out. And so, somehow, did Big Mike. Things he would sometimes say in the course of an ordinary conversation didn't blend with local opinion. They didn't have the colour of the recognized sacred tradition.

Sarah Coyne would give anything to know. She went to see him one Sunday night and she asked him straight out, did he or didn't he believe in God.

'I do,' he said, 'I believe in God. But I also believe in something deeper than God, something more divine the God.'

Backing away from the awful sincerity of the man, Sarah didn't ask him the further question that had come to mind. She didn't settle in for the long conversation she had imagined.

'It is hard on us getting used to you, Mike' she said, leaving. 'It is hard on all of us. But I helped to bring you into the world, Mike. Even before your mother did, I cupped your head in my hands, so I have maybe a right to tell you, we aren't as deeply keeled as you think we are. So don't let out too much sail to the wind, Mike. Don't let out too much sail to the wind.'

On land a man can run the risk of being an individual. He can find his own way of cutting the turf. On land a man can be himself, with or against the traditional way. On the ocean, no. At nightfall the moment four men step off the pier into their boat, the moment they fix their oars in their hole pins and start pulling, leaving their moorings, at that moment whatever is individual and peculiar in them becomes submerged in a calm, collective, common rowing. Even if, out on the ocean on a wild night, the man in the bows makes a bad decision you will, till he recovers, row in with it, because four men rowing together have some chance, whereas four men rowing at cross purposes have no chance at all.

Manning the beam oars, Big Mike submerged himself in a common task. And maybe that's why, regularly now, he came to mass. Recognizing Jesus to be a good man at sea, he was willing to row in behind him.

And so it was that the women knew him, as they knew every other man, by the sound of his footsteps on the gravel path. And something in those sounds, a sense of silence sown by them, reassured Eilo Lacey.

It occurred in her, having talked to him one evening in his house, that maybe Big Mike was a holy man.

But how could this be? How could a next-door neighbour of hers be any such thing?

Neither in appearance or behaviour did he resemble any of the saints she regularly prayed to.

He didn't talk about holy things. And yet, when he talked about ordinary things, about tea or turf, it was like being at mass.

Could it be, she wondered, but only to herself, could it be that there is a kind of holiness Christianity has never recognized?

The thought threatened her. That thought put an end to all such thoughts. She would stay with what she knew. She would stay with the mass that Christ instituted and the priest celebrated.

By the end of March it was evident that Sarah Coyne was dying. She was dying hard, not willing to give in.

She asked Big Mike to sit with her at night.

Nine nights later he was still ministering to her, calmly, in word and deed.

In the end Sarah died in peace.

She had helped him to come into the world. He helped her leave it.

And people were sure of it. At her wake and at her funeral they were sure of it. They were sure that Big Mike had prepared her for whatever it was she would meet in eternity.

And now it wasn't only Eilo Lacey who was threatened by strange thoughts. All over again, everyone was having to get used to Big Mike.

Nor was that the end of it.

Having cleaned the nets one morning, he told Ned Lavelle that he wanted a break, so he wouldn't be manning the beam oars that night. This wasn't upsetting news for Ned. For the past couple of years his grandson, who had replaced Big Mike a few times, had been hoping for just such an opportunity.

That evening the women were aware of a vacancy, of something familiar not there, on the gravel path outside their doors, their doors to seaward. And again the next morning, it was by their absence that they were aware of Big Mike's footsteps.

It was like a bereavement, Nora McGrail thought. It was like an angel fallen silent.

One day, off and on all day, Ned Lavelle heard hammering up at Big Mike's house. Again the next day a few times he heard it.

What now, he wondered, what's he up to now?

Only one thing to do, he thought, I'll go and find out.

'You're not thinking,' he said, seeing what was afoot, 'you're not thinking, are you Mike, of going to sea in that one.'

'I was thinking that maybe I might,' Big Mike replied.

'Don't,' Ned said. 'Don't go to sea in a boat as ill-omened as she is. It isn't hearsay,' he said. 'I was there myself that day. I saw it myself. She was standing there, perfect and finished, a beautiful thing. Proud of her, the boatwright tapped her lightly on the right gunwale, and with a sudden, frightening crack, she split from stem to stem. A bad sign. A warning. Your grandfather heeded it. He left her to rot.'

People were at a loss what to think or do the evening Big Mike walked down to the pier and rowed himself out alone in all ill-omened boat into the ocean. Every door was next door that night. In houses three doors away, four doors away, from their own door is where everyone was sitting, talking, trying to comprehend. Everyone wanted to know what everyone else was thinking. What was he up to? Whatever it was, he wasn't respecting the ocean. He was tempting the ocean. He was breaking the bond, the understanding, between the people and the ocean.

Thou shalt not tempt the Lord thy God.

Thou shalt not tempt the ocean.

Thou shalt not tempt the immensities beyond the headland.

What else could it be? He didn't intend to come back. And now after every tide they would have to comb the foreshores looking for evidence of his drowning.

At daybreak they were waiting for the first boats to appear around the headland. Eagerly, as they came, they counted them – fifteen, sixteen, seventeen and yes, there it is, the eighteenth boat, they are all coming home, Big Mike is coming home.

He came home the next morning.

Morning after morning he came home like someone who had all his wits about him, he cleaned his nets, talked, as often as he would, about the drift and run of the sea, and then went home.

Whatever it was, it wasn't madness.

Yet again though, people were having to get used to him.

Three or four months later, having cleaned them one morning, he put his nets in a bag and took them home with him. Eilo Lacey who called to him, bringing eggs to him, later that morning, saw them hanging up outside in his outhouse.

Calling it a day, everyone said. Big Mike has called it a day.

Even the rocks seemed to breathe a sigh of relief.

And the women felt their prayers had been answered. They were glad. They wouldn't be coming home from the shore some morning with a washed-up sock or shoe.

They had reckoned only with their own hopes. Because there it was again that evening, the sound of his footsteps, Big Mike going down to the sea.

Three doors, four doors, five doors away from their own door you'd find them again that night, the people talking.

Gone out without nets!

There were no two ways about it.

The only question was, would it be classed as suicide, and if it was, where would they bury him? Given the currents, there was every chance that he would be washed up on this or on one of the neighbouring islands.

But no. Not yet.

In the morning, at first light, eighteen boats came round the headland. 'Let him be now,' John Joseph Burke said. 'Let him be. We don't know at all what ails him.'

Madness people could understand.

But this was worse than madness.

More dangerous altogether than madness.

Night after night, with no nets!

His nets hung up in a sack outside his outhouse, and yet, there he was rowing himself out every evening, out wide around the breakers, out around the headland into the ocean. For what?

There was no understanding it. As Mike Kane, doddering on two sticks, had advised them to do, they let him go. Even to pray for him now, some people felt, was somehow not right. Even if it ended up in disaster, even if you were the one who came across the washed-up shoe, so be it. Big Mike was gone beyond recall. Within himself, he was gone beyond the sound of the last foghorn, beyond the light of the last lighthouse.

And yet, for anyone who looked at him more than passingly, there was, very obviously, a kind of sanctity in him, and for anyone who listened, more than passingly, there was, in the sound of his footsteps now, a deep tranquility, a sense, as it were, of journey's end.

A man, gone beyond any lifeline Christianity could throw to him.

That's how it seemed.

And yet he might be a holy man.

Here on our island.

It was a terrifying thought.

'God bless you Big Mike,' Mike Kane said looking after him going down to the sea one evening. 'God bless you, Big Mike.'

A great forg came down over land and sea one night.

Steevie Ridge went to his door and looked out. He heard nothing. And you'd smell nothing, he called back to his wife, even with the snout of a fox you'd smell nothing tonight.

Julia Nec was Steevie's next-door neighbour.

Julia was blind. But Julia believed.

In the depths of her apron pocket she had a rosary beads. Those beads were her stars. They were her constellations.

It was in her apron pocket that Julia's firmament was. And in that firmament there were fifteen mysteries, five of them joyful, five of them sorrowful and five of them glorious.

Constellations to navigate by in time and eternity.

But when tonight Julia took them into her hand below in the depths of her apron pocket, she felt only darkness.

It was like the darkness that was before the world was.

Tonight, for the first time in her life, Julia had nothing to navigate by. Her faith was blind.

Oceanward also the darkness was serious.

Even if they could somehow shine out there tonight, the light of the human mind and the light of the human heart would be brighter extinguished.

Instinctively, on a night like this, fishermen row into the deep, and that's what they did.

Out there, in the deep, there are no breakers or headlands against which the ocean might roll them.

'Something ahead of us! Something ahead of us!' the man in the bow called out.

In unison, without thinking, all four rowers sheared away – away – away.

What in God's name can it be, Ned Lavelle thought. A whale or what!

And then, out of nowhere, like a slip of the tongue it was, he heard himself saying, 'Big Mike or what?'

Big Mike out here?

Could it be possible that it is out into this Great Deep he comes?

He called out,

'Is that you. Big Mike?'

'Is that you. Big Mike?'

And the answer came back.

'It is.'

'It's me.'

'It's Big Mike.'

'How's the fishing, Mike?'

'The fishing is good.'

'The fishing is very good.'

And from far, far away they heard him, all four of them heard him, Big Mike calling out,

'The fishing is good.'

'The fishing is very good.'

'The fishing, not fishing at all.'

'Is blessedness, is bliss.'

Eventually, there was light. To begin with, they couldn't determine whether it was the light of sunrise or of sunset. Hoping that it was sunrise, they rowed, but without much confidence, in its direction. In the end they found their bearings and rowed home. Big Mike, in his boat alone, rowing behind them.

It was more than Ned Lavelle could take.

He got up and went up to Big Mike's house.

'What does it mean, Mike?'

'What in Christ's name does it mean? In the dark last night I called out asking you how the fishing was and in your voice, there is no mistaking your voice, Big Mike, in your voice, all four of us, hearing you, you answered, "The fishing is good, the fishing is very good, the fishing, not fishing at all, is blessedness, is bliss." I looked in your boat, moored below at the pier this morning, and there wasn't a fish-scale in it. What are you up to, Big Mike?'

'It's a long story, Ned. Living it or being lived by it, it was long. I wasn't long at sea when one night keeping watch before the mast I heard a sound. It wasn't an everyday sound and it wasn't in my everyday hearing I heard it. Hearing it, I knew that something at once wonderful and terrible had happened. All I could say about it is that, ever so briefly, while it lasted, I wasn't in the world. Either my world had vanished or my awareness of it had vanished, or maybe they had vanished together, and there it was, the sound, the first pure sound out of the Divine Silence.

'For fear of blasphemy I'll say no more about it. I was never the same after that. The sailors sensed it. They said it was nerves. And I suppose outwardly, anyway, it was nerves, for I had lost all sense of inner individual grounding, of grounding in selfhood, and I hadn't yet found grounding in God. Inwardly, I was in an awful no-man's-land, or no-man's-void, between ground lost and ground not yet found. During all those years though, deep within me, I was a kind of praying, a kind of speechless praying. I was, if you like, a dumfounded state of prayer. And then at last, to give it a chance, I would sometimes go inland, spending weeks on end in monasteries in India and China, in Hindu monasteries in India, and in Taoist monasteries in China. But even in them there wasn't the kind of silence I was seeking, and one day, in the Australian outback, an old medicine man advised me to go home, and that's why, one evening after thirty years, there was smoke from this chimney. From then on it was like being Job, it was like being Jonah. And like Job and like Jonah, I had to let God enact a parable on me. I had to become a living parable. A Truth that God would make visible be made visible in me.

'Night after night, alone in an unlucky boat, I rowed myself out, out wide around the breakers, out around the headland, into the ocean. Out there, night after night, I cast the net of my mind into the ocean of experience. Into it also I cast the net of my heart. Every morning, hauling the net of my mind, I hoped that in it I would find the great creed, the great knowing. But I never did. Neither did I, hauling the net of my heart, find in it the great emotion, the great saving passion or rapture. In both nets, from time to time, I found marvels. But I didn't find final healing.

'Final healing isn't healing of the mind, nor is it healing of the heart. It is healing beyond them, into Divine Ground. Divine Ground within.

Divine Ground below passion and love in the human heart, below knowing in the human mind.

'You know the rest.

'The net of my mind and the net of my heart hung up in a bag outside in my outhouse, I rowed myself out, and it's true Ned, it's true.

> Out there, in that Divine Dark,
> Out there, in that Divine Deep,
> The fishing is good,
> The fishing is very good.
>
> Out there, in that Divine Dark,
> Out there, in that Divine Deep,
> The fishing, not fishing at all,
> Is blessedness, is bliss.'

(Turtle, Vol. 1, pp. 213–21)

It was after closing time and Martin was proud of God.

'That's the long and the short of it now,' he declared, 'I'm proud of God.'

I managed him up the steps. We were almost at the door when he stopped, elaborately, not going a foot farther.

'Give me your hand,' he said.

'Lave it there,' he said.

'My besht friend,' he said.

'The coldesht day in winter,' he said, 'and the hottesht day in summer.'

Knowing that I wasn't appeased, he looked up at me forlornly:

'No use hangn a man without a head, John. No use hangn a man without a head.'

'No, Martin, no.'

No.

I managed him through the hall door, out into the night.

Even in the dark he was proud of God. 'Thanks be to God and his Blessed Mother, we had a hishtoric booze. Thanks be to dh'Almighty Redeemer we had a brave talk, in brave company, and John! Do you know John, I'd shtand naked in the shnow lishtnen to that one. A lovely girl she was, John. A lovely girl and a grand girl and sure tishnt from the wind she took it, don't I know all belongn to her for four generations back.'

'The song she sang, John, sing that song.'

I sang one verse:

> 'And how proud was I of my girl so tall,
> I was envied mostly by young men all
> When I brought her blushing, with bashful pride,
> To my cottage home by Loch Shileann side.'

'Lave it there,' he said, shaking my hand.

''Twas a hishtoric booze, wazhnt it, John?'

''Twas Martin, 'twas.'

Shaking my hand, he assured me again, whatever the weather, he would be with me. On the coldesht day in winter he'd be with me. With me, if I needed him, on the hottesht day of summer.

We made it as far as the stand of trees. He wanted a smoke. We sat down.

Holding the lighted match vertically for a moment, it bloomed into an unflickering, perfect flame. It didn't illuminate the dark. Making way for it, the darkness of this dark December night withdrew from a brief distraction it had no need of.

And I wondered: would the universe be a brief distraction to it also?

Drawing hard on his pipe, having with difficulty put the lid on it, he retrieved, as much from his suddenly beneficent memory as from his overcoat pocket, the half bottle of whiskey he had bought.

I knew we'd be here for a long time.

Having oilskins on, I lay back on the leaf-strewn, twig-strewn earth under the trees, lime trees and chestnuts.

Come next April, this will be a sea of daffodils, I thought. A sea, it will sometimes seem, of yellow consciousness. In comparison, the consciousness with which we run the world, the consciousness we have settled for, will seem dull and grey. Can we believe Hindus and Buddhists? I wondered. Deep down in our inner-soil, in our thought-strewn, dream-strewn, desire-strewn soil, are there, deep down in us, bulbs of other kinds of consciousness? Bulbs that, given a chance, would bloom like Martin's match? Bloom in our darkness? Lotuses of other kinds of consciousness, crimson consciousness, sapphire-blue consciousness, blooming in the aqueous and vitreous humours of our eyes. I thought of the water lilies in the lake above at Lisnabrucka, their roots in the mud, their stems reaching up through the water, their blossoms in sunlight. Is it possible, I wondered, that I've never risen above the mud? When will my chakras open?

'You ha' me kilt John,' Martin said. 'You ha' me kilt. Never once have I seen you at the holy mass in Roundstone, and you a grand man and a fine man and a great neighbour. You ha' me kilt, not believn in God, man or the divel.'

'All whom it may concern,' he said, 'All whom it may concern …'

I knew that whatever it was it was intended to particularly concern me.

'There was a man down Carna way one day, John, sittn on the sea-wall he was, smokn his pipe. A tourisht car came along and shtopt and the man who was drivn rolled down the window and ashkt, "Am I on the right road to Carna?" The Carna man took his pipe out of his mouth, he looked up the road and down the road and then, lookn at your man in the car, he said, "You are, yeh, you're on the right road to Carna, but you're turnt the wrong way."'

'I'm on the right road alright, Martin. That's what you're telling me isn't it? I'm on the right road to heaven but, and 'tis a big "but", isn't it, Martin, I'm turnt the wrong way.'

''Tis against your own feet you're walking, Martin.' I was trying to manage him across the cattle trap at end of the avenue.

'Whisht,' he said. 'Whisht, John. God bless you, John, your one way is one way but I can't help it if my one way wants to be every way?'

Awkwardly, all ways, we crossed over.

'I'm as drunk as a nine-wheel cart, John.'

'I know, Martin.'

Eyesight in this kind of darkness was a bad habit. Wholly ineffective though it was, it nonetheless distracted attention from hearing and touch – from information coming to us through our feet.

'Where are we, John?'

'On the back road.'

'Where's that?'

'At Ballynahinch.'

'Ballynahinch!'

'Yeh.'

'The corns is kilin me.'

Knowing what this meant, I ignored the remark.

'Not long till Christmas, Martin.'

'Christmas!'

'Yes.'

'I'm lamed, John.'

Having pity for him, but against my will, I groped my way, groping the air, to the side of the road and I sat him down on a low wall. I sat down myself.

'Where are we?'

'At the stable.'

'The shtables.'

'Yes.'

'God be with dh'oul shtables. God be with dh'oul shtables. Many and many and many is the fine bucket of fine cow's milk Ted and mesel milked in them oul shtables. Ted and mesel. Ted and mesel. The Lord have mercy on Ted, the Lord have mercy of Ted, the Lord have mercy on Ted – say it, you son of a bitch, say it.'

'The Lord have mercy on Ted.' I said promptly.

The thought of it, Ted dead and buried below in Carna, it was all too much for him. He took to the bottle.

Given how much the mood had changed, it was a sob of light that bloomed from his matchstick now. Briefly perfect, it died on its way to the bowl of his pipe.

And the whiskey wasn't helping.

'Wings I thought twould give me, John. But no. Fins it gave me. The fins of an eel it gave me. I'm an eel in a boghole, John.'

Is there, I wondered, thinking of Martin and me sitting there on a low wall in front of the old stables, is there a desolation that is independent of us? A desolation of the time or of the place. A desolation of the night. Up the road it had come and here we were, our mood inexplicably changed. We had a pipe, a sob of light, and a whiskey bottle. And we had two antiphons, the first being, the coldesht day in winter and the hottesht day in summer, the second being, no use hangn a man without a head.

It was our midnight mass. Our mass for the dead.

It was our mass for all that was dead in ourselves.

It was our mass for the bulbs that never sprouted in us.

It was our mass for the sea of yellow consciousness

That never bloomed in us.

Kyrie eleison
Kyrie eleison
Kyrie eleison

No use hanging a man without a head.
No use hanging a man without a head.
No use hanging a man without a head.

No, not on a night as dark as this.

And it wasn't yet a destitute dark. Or a bereaved dark.

It didn't yearn to be sown with stars. A sense I had, walking beside the most silent reach of the Owenmore river, is that the metaphysical is sensuous, so sensuous that, its presence once felt, hearing, seeing, touch, taste and smell swoon away, knowing themselves to be empty distractions.

It occurred to me, crossing Lowry's Bridge, that we needed a hymn tonight. But I didn't give it much thought, because, here in Connemara tonight, Night was having its Easter. We were walking in an Easter of darkness. An Easter of Divine Darkness. The dark as it was before it was trivialized by starlight and sunlight.

'Happy Easter, Martin.'

'Are you there, John?'

'I am, Martin.'

'Where are we?'

'At Lowry's Bridge.'

'I'm as drunk as a nine-wheel cart, John.'

'Me too, Martin. Me too. I'm as drunk as the nine-wheel cart that has come for to carry us home.'

Coming out onto the road to Derrada, Martin wanted to go left.

'No, Martin, no,' I said. 'That's the way to Ballinafad.'

He erupted. No whorin Kerryman would tell him the way home.

'Don't I know the place like the back of my hand. Washnt it here, right here at six o'clock one morning, that I met my father and mother, me comin from a wedding or a wake in Emiaghmore, and them, the two of them, drivn two cows before them to the auld cow's fair in Clifden. John! God bless you John, the random is on you …'

It was a long argument.

In the end, taking command, I stood him in the middle of the road and said, 'Now, Martin, that's your right ear, isn't it? And in it you can hear the sound of the Owenmore river, can't you? And knowing this place as well as you do, knowing it like the back of your own hand, you know that the road along the river is the road to Derrada, you know that, don't you, Martin?'

Having won the argument, I felt sorry for him. Hoping it would mollify him, I reminded him of the song the young woman had sung. I knew he would ask me to sing it. I sang it.

A HUT AT THE EDGE OF THE VILLAGE

Fare thee well old Ireland, a long farewell,
My bitter anguish no tongue can tell,
For I'm going to cross the ocean wide
From my cottage home by Loch Shileann side.

At the village dance by the Shannon stream,
Where Blind O'Leary enchantments played,
No harp like his could so cheerily play
And no one could smile like my Eileen gay.

And how proud was I of my girl so tall,
I was envied mostly by young men all,
When I brought her blushing with bashful pride
To my cottage home by Loch Shileann side.

But alas! our joy twas not meant to last,
The landlord came our sweet home to blast
And he to us would no mercy show
And he turned us out in the blinding snow.

And no one to us would then open their door,
Oh God! your justice it was rich and sore,
For my Eileen fainted in my arms and died
As the snow fell down by Loch Shileann side.

Then I raised my hands to the heavens above,
I said a prayer for my life's lost love,
Oh God of Justice, I loudly cried,
Revenge the death of my murdered bride.

Then I hid her down in the churchyard low
Where in the springtime sweet daisies grow;
I shed no tears for my eyes were dry

IN THAT DIVINE DARKNESS, THE FISHING WAS GOOD

As the snow fell down by the graveyard side

So fare thee, well old Ireland, fare thee well, adieu,
My ship is taking me away from you,
But where e'er I wander my thoughts will bide
At my Eileen's grave by Loch Shileann side.

'Enchantments played,' Martin said, lingering as though he were himself enchanted by every syllable. We had a new antiphon:

en-chantments-played!
en-chantments-played!

Our midnight mass was growing.

We had already crossed Dervikrune Bridge when a sheep coughed on the side of Derrada Hill.

'What ails you?'

'Nothing Martin. Nothing. Twas a sheep that coughed.'

'One of Petey's sheep?'

'Yes.'

'Hooze, I suppose.'

'Or fluke?'

'Fluke. Musht be fluke.'

He stopped, his head bowed. 'The Lord have mercy on Petey,' he said. 'The Lord have mercy on Petey.'

'Yes,' I said, instantly, 'the Lord have mercy on Petey.'

'Petey Welsh!' he said. 'A great neighbour was Petey. Petey was up there on Derrada Hill one day, a hill he walked every day, after sheep, but this day, no matter how hard he tried, he couldn't come down out of it. Thinkn he had maybe stepped on a *fóidín mearaí* he took off his coat, turned it inside out, put it back on, and now, with the greatest ease in the world, he found his bearings, walked down the hill and in his own door.'

'*Fóidín mearaí* you call it, Martin?'

'That's what it's called, the sod of confusion, the sod of bewilderment. 'Tis well known they are out there, such sods. Shtep on one of them and you'll wander around bewildered and confused all night till the Moon comes up, or you'll wander around, the random on you, till you take off your coat and put it back on, inside out.'

'Even if we take off our natures and put them back on inside out I don't think we'll reach home tonight, not at the rate we're going, Martin.'

He didn't answer.

'How are you, Martin?

'Never better. And yourself?'

'Fine, Martin, fine.'

'My besht friend John. Lave it there,' he said, breaking free from me.

'Lave it there,' he said, shaking my hand. 'The coldesht day in winter and the hottesht day in summer.'

'That's right, Martin.'

''Tis, John, 'tis.'

'The river has a lovely name, hasn't it, Martin?'

'The river?'

'Yes.'

'You mean the Owenmore?'

'Yes. The long, long flowings and the little falls of the Owenmore.'

'The Owenmore?'

'Yes, Martin.'

'The long, long flowings and the little falls of the Owenmore would be soul to someone who came here having no soul at all.'

'No soul at all?'

'I had no soul at all, none that I was aware of, when I came here, Martin.'

'What was that?'

'A salmon, Martin. A salmon leaped.'

'A salmon? '

'Yes.'

'Salmon is whores, John. Ted and Mickey and Josey and mesel was up here poaching one night. We set the nets but then the thunder came, three or four big rolls of it and that was it. We knew that was it. We went home without a shcale. You know that, don't you? Salmon sink to the bottom when there's thunder. On a night of thunder t'would take an otter to frighten them out of their lie, into the nets.'

'How are you, Martin?'

'Not good. To tell you the Christ's truth I'm not good. I'm by no means good. 'Tis like being blind.'

'Should we turn our coats inside out?'

'No.'

'No.'

'No. No use. Where are we?'

'At the quarry.'

'I don't believe it. We're at the quarry, Martin.'

'I'll not believe it.'

'It's alright, Martin.'

'We could be somewhere awful.'

'We could be, Martin, but we aren't. We're passing the quarry.'

'You're shtubbom.'

''Tis you that's shtubborn, Martin.'

'We'll sit down.'

'No, Martin no, we won't.'

'We'll wait for morning.'

'We won't, Martin. God bless you, Martin, God bless you and spare you, but try to keep walking. We'll make it, Martin.'

'We're losht!'

'We aren't.'

'Where are we?'

'We're at the quarry.'

'I see no quarry.'

'Alright, Martin, alright,' I said. I stood him now again in the middle of the road. 'Can you hear the river, Martin? Can you hear the near roaring? That's the roaring at the eel weir. And the roaring farther on, can you hear that farther roaring, that's the roaring at Ted's place. Below Ted's place is Lynn's place, below Lynn's place is my place. Around the corner from my place is Petey Welsh's place. And up the bohreen from Petey Welsh's place is your place.'

'Places! Places! Places! You have me mesmerized with places!'

'Where are we?'

I faced him towards the quarry wall, or what I presumed was the quarry wall, and I told him to look straight ahead.

Staggering forward a little, he stood there, his hands resting on his knees, peering into the void. He was looking hard. I could sense how hard he was looking. He looked for a long while. At last, recognizing something, he half called, half wailed, 'John! Are you there, John? Are you there, John? Oh John, sure I know well where we're now, John. I know well where we're now, John. But where! the fuck! are we?'

Sitting by my revived fire, having left Martin home, I attempted, if only initially, to come to terms with Martin's answer.

Is the whole world, I wondered, a *fóidín mearaí*? Is every lobe of the human mind, dreaming and waking, a *fóidín mearaí*? And the easy assurance we almost always have of knowing where we are in terms of our whereabouts, is that, because it is so unsuspected, the most serious of all our bewilderments? I imagined it this way: asleep one night, here in my house in Derrada West, I slip into a dream. In the dream I experience myself to be in Iran, walking in arid country south of Isfahan. A man who comes towards me asks me, where am I? A few miles from Isfahan in Iran, I say, pointing to the blue dome of the Majis-I-Shah mosque. While my hand is still pointing I wake up and to my astonishment I'm not in Iran at all but in my room in Derrada West.

Waking up from dreaming. Waking up from waking.

Waking up from waking I realize that I'm not in a universe at all. I'm in the void. The void that is void of worldly reality. Cartographers of the universe are cartographers of that void. And so it is that I imagine myself talking to a modern astronomer, Carl Sagan, say.

IN THAT DIVINE DARKNESS, THE FISHING WAS GOOD

'Astronomers have been looking at the universe for a long time now, Carl. During the last three centuries ye have been looking at it through optical telescopes and, more recently, ye have been listening to it through radio telescopes. Could you tell me, where are we?'

'Well,' I imagine Carl saying, 'the universe is composed of galaxies. Some of these galaxies are in clusters called mega galaxies. One of these galaxies is called the Milky Way. It is a spiral galaxy. It has a 100 million stars in it. On the outer arm of the spiral there is a star that we call the Sun. Circling about that Sun are nine planets. The third planet out is called the Earth. That's where we are.'

To which I reply, 'Are you there, Carl? Are you there, Carl? Oh! Sure I know well where we're now, Carl. I know well where we are now, but, knowing where we are in terms of our whereabouts, what kind of knowing is that? One day, waking up from waking, you will find yourself pointing at the void.'

The only antiphons I was left with going to bed were

> enchantments played,
> enchantments played,
> *fóidín mearaí,*
> *fóidín mearaí.*

Lying there, too frightened to fall asleep, I calmed and consoled myself with a Hindu parable:

Narada was a solitary. So altruistically motivated was he in his long and perilous quest for the Truth, that one day it was Vishnu the great God, the great Mayin himself, who was standing in his door.

'Conscious of all that you have endured on behalf of all things,' Vishnu said, 'I have come to grant you the boon of your choice.'

'The only boon I have ever wished for,' Narada replied, 'is to understand the secret of your maya. It will please me, Holy One, if you show me the source, and the power over us, of the World illusion.'

As if to dissuade him, Vishnu smiled, strangely. But, having named his boon, Narada remained silent.

'Come with me,' Vishnu said, his strange smile not fading. Before long the arid land they were walking in had turned into a terrible, red desert. Moisture in their mouths was turning to ashes. Like the cracked rocks their minds were cracking.

Claiming he could go no farther, Vishnu sat down.

Seeking water for his God, Narada struggled on. To his great delight the desert gave way to scrubland, the scrubland gave way to sown land and then, in a valley below him, there it was, a lovely green village.

He knocked on the first door. So enchantingly beautiful was the young woman who opened it that he instantly and entirely forgot what it was he had come for. It was strange. As if this house had always been his home he sat and ate with the family. Early next morning he was working in their fields with them. At seed-sowing he worked. At harvest he worked. In the quiet time between seasons he asked her father if he might have the young woman's hand in marriage. Three children were born to them, and when the old man died Narada became head of the household.

One year the monsoon rains were like the rains at the end of a world. Night or day there was no let up. The river burst its banks and struggling one night to reach the safety of the higher ground, Narada's wife was swept away. Wailings in the chaos of the waters was the last he heard of his three children. He was swept away himself but, miraculously, not to drowning. He was sitting on a hill. So terrible and red was the glare he couldn't open his eyes. Moisture in his mouth was turning to ashes. Like the cracked rocks, his sanity was cracking. Then, from behind him, he heard a voice, familiar but enigmatic: 'I've been waiting for almost a half an hour now, did you bring the water?'

Our Hindu parable.
Our Hindu

> Ite, missa est.
> *Go, you are sent forth.*

From O'Leary's enchantments and from Vishnu's enchantments.
From Loch Shileann and the Green Village.
From Ireland and the World Illusion.
From the *fóidín mearaí*.

Too disturbed to sleep, I retrieve *The Dark Night of the Soul* by St John of the Cross from beneath my pillow:

> In what fear in danger then must man be living, seeing that the very light of his natural eyes, by which he directs his steps, is the very first to bewilder and deceive him when he would draw near unto God. If he wishes to be sure of the road he travels on, he must close his eyes and walk in the dark, if he is to journey in safety from his domestic foes, which are his own senses and faculties.

Like Narada, I had stepped off the *fóidín mearaí* and that was as dangerous as it was when, innumerable incarnations earlier, I had first set foot on it.

'No use hanging a man without a head, Martin.'

'No.'

'No use hanging a man without a head.'

The spell was broken and now, like the skull at the foot of the cross, I could hear the God, himself crucified, asking the question:

'I thirst. Did you bring the water?'

(*Turtle, Vol. 1*, pp. 202–12)

In That Divine Deepness, the Fishing Was Good

— *On Story* —

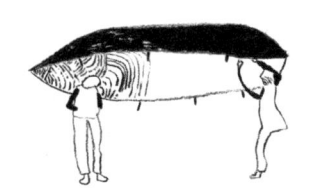

Behind most complaint, jubilation or grief dwells a fairy tale. Behind most consternation, bafflement or fear dwells a myth. As we return to Moriarty's relationship to story, we are lifted from personal tales into the realm of folktale, legend and magic. The connective tissue is far closer than we think. There is this orality to John's tellings – the sense of chant I go on about – that comes from a chewing of the stories in the jaw, not just immediately committing to page. There is a danger of weightlessness when that occurs. Much of what waits in an old story requires spit and bright mind to commingle before it reveals itself.

John's oral surety as a storyteller kicks the stories along beautifully, humanely, but his skill as a mythologist provokes the subtlest extractions. Amongst some storytellers, this is a kind of heresy; the story should do all the speaking for itself, thank you very much. Well, if we were in a half-mythically literate culture then that may do well for us. That we would catch each inflection and implication immediately. But we are not. We are woefully divorced from that ground. It is good that John meditates on the tales. He is demonstrating an almost forgotten tongue, and he rescues many wisps of image we may otherwise step over. Moriarty's capacities as an associative mythographer are rather out of style these days.

The myths are a constant unfolding for John, an endless, companionable hermeneutics; not a map, not an ABC, but an atmosphere, a discipline, a way of beholding circumstance, a way of beholding consciousness.

The old belief is that these stories are not just a human mantra of anxiety over death and mystery, but a chattering jungle of many calls and cries. The perspectives in a tale are not always hearth-fire ruminations . This is where the most irresistible sense of ecology rises. It seems the myths could possibly arise from the land, not the landowner. Abandon myth and you receive its often troubled brother, nationalism.

To prompt an image Moriarty used, these stories are seal holes where we receive messages behind animal and human, weather pattern and ancestor, the gods and the beloveds, all chattering back and forth.

I

Other boys had an ancestry, I had a pedigree, and my pedigree meant it was mostly through dreaming that I would know and deal with reality. Overflowing all inner and outer banks, dreaming would sometimes be an inundation, an outcrop of waking nowhere in sight.

Even when he was near me, talking to me, my father was far away. In birdform, among birds, their underwings raucously red, is how I remember him.

Meass Buachalla was my mother. She looked after a king's cattle. She had cures. And she crossed into Otherworlds as easily as someone who has slept all night crosses into waking. Sometimes a long sojourn in an Otherworld would fall between the two parts of a conversation I'd have with her.

The birds my father flocked with could, on occasion, be murmuringly savage. Mostly, though, they were as shy as geese. Only once did I ever come close to them. Which was my father I couldn't say. When they took flight, I saw again that underwing and underweb they were raucously red.

One evening, shortly before I'd have closed it, a hurt bird, a skald crow, flew through my door. Without thinking, I held out my hand, palm downwards. She perched on it. She looked at me. She squawked three times. Then she flew back out, leaving her hurt behind. I knew I would carry that hurt for the rest of my life. And I also knew that I wouldn't be a warrior, even though that's why I had been fostered out so young to my uncle, a wide man, a man of war, and famous, his hospitality talked of from sea to sea.

After seven years I had only my hurt to go home with. And I didn't reach home.

The path I had taken was taking me nowhere. Mountains I had in mind, it hadn't in mind. 'Twas as if it were walked only by beings who had no knowledge or need of elsewhere. Are there such beings? I wondered. I was beginning to be frightened. Are there beings for whom all elsewheres are where we are? What kind of mind have they? What kind of eyes?

At the end of three vexed days, the sunset vexed and very red, I gave up. I sat on a rock. It was strange. These thoughts I was thinking didn't seem to be my thoughts. But whose thoughts were they? Were they the land's thoughts? It was an old, old land, older than human intentions and purposes. Human intentions and purposes were nowhere visible in it. Was it taking me over? Was it thinking through me?

Could it be, I thought, that I have walked into a mood of mind or a mood of nature in which there are no intentions? Could it be, I thought, that having intentions fences me in?

But thoughts like these couldn't be my thoughts.

Thoughts like these didn't fit my forehead. They didn't fit seed or sense in me. I was afraid. Had I walked into someone's dream of me?

I got up and walked on, looking for evidence of the eveday world.

It was everywhere in evidence.

Off the path, on a patch of wet grass, was a pair of snails. Copulating they were, their horns, all eight of them, withdrawn from the distractions of a world now not necessary.

In the lee of a shag of bushes, mostly blackthorn, not yet blossoming, was a ram.

Lying there, his head high, he was chewing the cud and between his horns, leaning forward, a magpie was picking wool for her nest.

As I approached it, noisily, a stick breaking under my feet, a pair of mallard broke in a frightened confusion of forms from a cove of reeds and then, assuming distinct duck shapes, they turned south and the water drops that fell from them left trails of expanding circles on the candour of the lake.

Three days became four days.

Three nights became four nights.

After nine days and nights I knew that, disarmed as I was, I had met my destiny. The candour of the lake in front of me, that was it.

It was a temptation to something more dangerous than sanctity.

Leaving her hurt in me, the hurt bird had disarmed me of shield and spear and sword. Had disarmed me of high horsemanship, of a right, already won, to a high place at the warrior's table.

But now the lake was disarming me, not of accoutrements and acquirements, but of something I was. And nine years later, having lived since then in a restored crannog, a high island to the north of me, patches of reeds east of me, nine years later it would still, at odd moments, disarm me of all I self seekingly was.

I would see how unworldly the world was.

There were mornings, calm and clear, when the candour of the lake was candour of hand and eye in me.

The candour of its seeing would sometimes be my seeing, seeing the mountains without distortion.

The distortion of greed.
The distortion of anger.
The distortion of love.
The distortion of hope.
The distortion of despair.
The distortion above all of intention and purpose.

At night, delight was the light in my lamp, it was the light in me. And moths came. A moth from Brí Leith.

It was her joy to find someone with whom she could be human. It was her joy to find someone who was able for the splendours of her needs at night. It was hurt in me that enabled me. We pitied the shining stars. But we knew, looking at them, that their night would come. It had come for us. All summer long all elsewheres were where we were. Tír Tairngrí was in her hair. Magh Meall was in my eyes. We walked, whenever we walked abroad, in Emain Abhlach.

II

I dreamed: my house was my grave mound. I was desolate, groping carved walls in the darkness. I found the passage. I was walking, I hoped, towards dawn. A solstice spear, a Sun-spear, speared me, tumbling me back on to the sepulchral floor.

I sat with the bones of my incarnations.

I ate the food of the dead. Bird food, boar food, horse food. Someone was there.

He was gathering the bones. Bones of the bird I was, of the boar I was, of the horse I was. Of creatures unknown that I was.

He heaped them together, boar bones at the bottom, bird bones on top. 'Your bonefire,' he said, setting fire to them.

He threw me into the flames.

I was sitting in ashes when I revived.

My first breath was a last plume of smoke.

'Eat it,' he said.

As I ate the ashes, I had visions. I was walking with animals. I was kind of their kind. I was mind of their mind. I woke up. I got up. Crossing the causeway I was when I realized I had the Sun-spear in my hand. It would, I realized, be in my hand whenever I needed it.

III

In a wood a voice called out.

> You are now a people's dream of you. Walk in it.

Again, after a long while, it called,

> Walk in it.

Six mornings later before sunrise it called,

> Walk in the people's dream of you.

The last time it called the voice was an echo:

> Naked, it said, naked naked naked.

Naked, like a child not ashamed, I walked out of the wood. Ahead of me, on the rough sward, grazing it, were the birds my father flocked with.

I walked towards them. They took to flight alighting not far away. I kept walking. Again they took flight, and again they alighted. And so it continued till they came to the sea. There the one who was my father turned and, assuming human form, he came to me saying, 'Walk on as you are. Walk northwards naked to Tara. You will be king.'

IV

He could escape into other species, she could escape into other worlds. I couldn't. Or rather I decided that even if I could I wouldn't. Smoke of a bonefire in my nostrils, Magh Meall long gone from my eyes, I would be loyal to the hurt human, the hurt bird. My reign would be a Birdreign.

Walking northwards naked to Tara, a Sun-spear, spear of initiations, in my hand, that was my people's dream of me. That was Étain's dream of me. Throughout all my reign Étain was human. Étain was happy.

And Manannán mac Lir, he was happy one night to find Ireland, not Tír Tairngrí, in Fand's hair.

AFTERTHOUGHTS

Cometh the hour, cometh Conaire Mór, a man willing to walk in nature's dream of him, in his people's dream of him. Reaching Tara, the savagely insurgent chariot accepted him, the royal mantle fitted him, Blocc and Bluigne, the druidic standing stones, opened before him, and, riding past it, Fál the stone phallus screeched against his chariot axle. Also, in a seriously sacred rite called the Bainis Rí, he married Meadhbh the goddess of sovereignty.

Unlike Christ, Conaire doesn't take the hurt of the world upon himself but, the exceptional hurt the skald crow left him with, that he accepts.

As tall and as wide as himself, that hurt, that wound, is the opening through which he walks out into an exceptional destiny. In accepting the wound he accepted the destiny.

Lakes unruffled by legend, the two lakes in Glendalough and Lough Derravaragh, these lakes Conaire matched in candour, and in this, ever before he was king, he was royal.

Unlike the Fisher King, it is creatively that Conaire is maimed and so it is that he can lie with a woman in the splendours of their needs, his needs and her needs, at night.

It is only in killing him regeneratively with it that the Sun, itself regenerated now at the winter solstice, can give the Sun-spear to Conaire.

Having been killed regeneratively by it, Conaire can launch the sun-spear in the knowledge, sure and serene, that he will not be contaminated by the evil that he must oppose.

Walking north to what is royal in himself, Conaire's road becomes the Road of Ashes. The ashes of all his incarnations, past, present and to come.

For now he walks naked. Naked of accoutrements, naked of kind.

Individual and particular though he is, Conaire walking naked to Tara is all of us walking naked to Tara. Conaire walking naked to what is royal in himself is all of us walking naked to what is royal in ourselves.

In inhaling a last wisp of smoke rising from the bonefire of his incarnations, Conaire is showing himself able to acknowledge and inherit all that he has been, is showing himself able not only to coexist but to coincide with his shadow.

Having integrated it as perfectly as he has, Conaire's shadow isn't for projecting onto things. To Conaire, things are things not masks of his repressions.

It is what Conaire as king represents, the democracy of being regeneratively speared, the democracy of being reduced to ashes in the bonefire, the democracy of walking north to what is royal in us, the democracy of being right royal.

And yes, it delights Étain to be human, to have it in her to experience the limitless geographies of love and the all too unplentiful pit of despair.

Having suffered so many shapeshifts, having lived so variously, as fox, as moth, as owl, as trout, Étain's is a naturally ecumenical humanity.

As is Conaire's. Ecumenical with all that he inwardly is, it comes naturally to Conaire to be ecumenical with everything around him.

Totemic as they are to each other, everything we say of Conaire we can say of the bird. That's why his reign is called

The Birdreign

Ingcél and Fer Rogain talk about it in an early medieval text called Togail Bruidne Dá Derga, or The Destruction of Dá Derga's Hostel:

'Cid ahé libse a flaithius ind fir sin i tír nÉrenn?' or Ingcél.

'Is maith a flaith,' ol Fer Rogain. 'Ní taudchaid nél tar gréin ó gabais flaith ó medón erraich co medón fogmair, ocus ní taudchaid banna drúchtae di feór co medón lai, ocus ní fascnan gaemgaeth cairchech cethrae co nónae, ocus ní foruich mac tibhri ina flaith tar ag fireand cacha indise ón chind mbliadnae co araill. Ocus ataat secht meic thiri i ngiallnai fri raigid ina thigseom fri coimét in rechtai sin ocus atá cúlaitiri iarna cúl .i. Macc Locc ocus is é taccair tar a cend hi tig Conaire. Is ina flaith is combind la cach fer guth araili ocus betis téta mendchrot ar febus na cána ocus in tsída ocus in cháinchomraic fil sethnu na Hérind. Is ina flaith ataat na trí bairr for Érind .i. barr dés ocus barr scoth ocus barr measa.'

'What,' asked Ingcél, 'are the virtues of his reign in Ireland?'

'A good reign it is,' replied Fer Rogain. 'Since he became king no cloud covers the Sun from the middle of spring until the middle of autumn and not a drop of dew evaporates from the grass till midday and no gust of wind shakes a cow's tail till evening and in any one year a wolf will take only one bull calf from an enclosure and in guarantee of this agreement seven wolves remain as hostages by the wall of his house and, by way of further assurance, Mac Locc pleads their case in Conaire's house. To his neighbour each man's voice is as melodious as the strings of harps and that because of the excellence of law and of peace and goodwill that is now to be found throughout Ireland. It is in Conaire's reign that we have the three crowns of Ériu, the crown of corn, the crown of flowers and the crown of acorns.'

How it was in Ireland during *Ind Énflaith*

during *The Birdreign*

FURTHER REFLECTIONS

Cormac and Conaire. Each in his own way, they undertake or rather they undergo the hazardous journey to Tara.

Dreamed by their people on to that road, each of them is a king in the making.

In the sense that it engages us in the roots of who we are, this road to our royalty is a root road, as it were an etymological road. Beset by our totem ancestors, whether wolf or bear or bird, it is a primary, if not primal, road. On it we are claimed as well by nature as by culture. On it we undergo our first shapeshiftingly insecure attempts to be human. To be totemically human, that is. For Cormac and Conaire on this road, safe assimilation to a totem animal outside themselves gives way to safe assimilation to animal nature in themselves. It is their attempt, in living it wholly, to bring the whole human psyche with them. That way, unlike Lughaidh mac Con, they won't be etymologically usurped.

Usurpation, totemic or otherwise, by animal nature from within, that is the hazard. Both Cormac and Conaire underwent and survived the hazard.

Realizing them vajrasatvically, making them vajrasatvically real, Cormac was struck by lightning and Conaire was made to pass through the fiercely destructive yet fiercely regenerating flames of the sepulchral bonefire.

Thinking of them, we can see that there is a higher totemism, the totemism of being assimilated not backwards to an archetype but forwards to a teleotype.

The word archetype is a compound of two Greek words, *arche*, meaning old in the creative sense of primary and original, and *tupos*, meaning a pattern of which copies are or can be made. Teleotype is also a compound of two Greek words, *teleos*, meaning perfect as applied to something fully realized and complete, and again *tupos*.

As fully realized human beings, royal in their natures before they were institutionally royal, Cormac and Conaire are teleotypes and, as such, we can aspire forward toward them, forward toward royal realization in ourselves on the day when, riding past it in Tara, the stone phallus will screech against our chariot axle. After the depredations and dislocations wrought in Ireland by Cromwell, two Kerry poets, Aodhghán Ó Rathaille and Eoghan Ruadh Ó Suilleabháin, dreamed of a restoration of the old Catholic, Gaelic order.

After centuries of ecological havoc we need a restoration of

Ind Énflaith

To Plato I say:

An Énflaith not a Republic, a thing too unetymologically and exclusively human to bring out the best in us. It doesn't suit us. Worse, it doesn't suit the Earth. And that, in the end, must mean Hell-upon-Earth.

To St Augustine I say:

Blocc and Bluigne, the druidic standing stones, have opened before us and we have passed through into a more or less druidic way of understanding ourselves and our world. In ourselves there is druidheacht. There is druidheacht in the world.

To Rousseau I say:

Listen to the screech out of Ireland. It is the screech of Fál, the stone phallus, announcing the universally ecumenical

IN THAT DIVINE DEEPNESS, THE FISHING WAS GOOD

Birdreign

To the blackbird who has just walked in through my open door and, having flown up onto it, stands unalarmed on a pile of books, among them a Cambridge Classics edition of *Oedipus Rex*, a king etymologically usurped – to him, the blackbird, I say:

that single screech of Fál is our universally ecumenical

Magna Carta

it is our universally ecumenical

Easter Proclamation

it is our universally ecumenical

Anthem

As for the feather the blackbird left behind – it could be a feather of

Maat

The goddess of Truth. Truth in the sense of

Right Cosmic Order

In our day it must mean what it once meant in Ireland:

A BIRDREIGN

A migration of the Western mind from Thebes to Tara, from the reign of our secretly insurgent repressions in Thebes to a reign inwardly and outwardly ecumenical at Tara – that would be real progress, wouldn't it?

To Plato we say, come live in

The Birdreign

To Rousseau we say, come live in

The Birdreign

To Karl Marx we say, come live in

The Birdreign

River and star and archaeornis and ammonite and wolf and bear and crab and crow and lichen and louse and oatgrass, aurora and oak, everything included, the good weal is a

Commonweal

Weal and woe.
Not without woe the

Commonweal

But, as the old book has it:

Bid saineamail ind énflaith

(*Invoking Ireland*, pp. 53–63)

In the mythic imagination of Indo-Europeans it is the great battle. In India it is the battle between the Devas and the Asuras. In Greece it is the battle between the Gods and the Giants. In Nordic countries it is the battle between the Aesir and the Vanir. In Ireland it is the battle between the Tuatha Dé Danann and the Fomorians.

An old book says this about the Tuatha Dé Danann:

Bátar Tuatha Dé Danann i n-indsib túascertachaib an domuin, aig foglaim fesa ocus fithnasachta ocus druidechtai ocus amaidechtai ocus amainsechta, combtar fortilde for súthib cerd ngenntlichtae.

Living as they then were in the northern islands of the world, the Tuatha Dé Danann spent their time acquiring visionary insight and foresight and hindsight, acquiring the occult knowledge and the occult arts of the wizard, the druid, the witch, these, together with all the magical arts, until, masters in everything concerning them, they had no equals in the world.

Little wonder then that it was in a great magical cloud that they came to Ireland, landing in the mountains of Conmaicne Re in Connacht. In truth they were a race of gods but, for all the occult arts at their command, it was their particular delight to be of one mind with the wind and the rain. Great warrior though he was, Ogma knew that a spear that went through him wouldn't open him out half as much to the Otherworld as the call of a curlew calling in a bog would open him out to this world. And Dien Cecht, their leech, he had the look of an upland thorn bush that has long ago yielded to the endless, night and day persuasions of the prevailing wind and is now no more than a current, than the memory of a current, in it.

In the end you could walk through the land and not know they were in it.

Their features hanging like seaweed when the tide is out, their tongues the colour and shape of cormorant's tongues, the clamour of ocean in their talk, Fomorians came ashore.

Forests cut down, rivers re-routed, towers everywhere, it was soon clear that it must come to a fight.

It did. In Magh Tuired.

Never before or since did the Battle Hag screech as she screeched that night, her mouth bleeding in excited anticipation of the greatest battle that would ever be fought in Ireland. So long and loud and piercing was her third screech, it cut gaps in the mountains, it sent the incoming tides back out and as far away as west Munster where a man was talking that night to his wife he didn't finish what he had to say because, sliced down the middle, the two halves of him and of what he was saying fell either side of her.

It was that kind of battle.

As much because of what their wizards did as what their warriors did, victory was with the Tuatha Dé Danann, or so it seemed.

When the outcome was still in doubt Mathgen, their chief wizard, went chanting forward and so burning a thirst did he cause not just the mouths but in the minds of the fighting Fomorian warriors that, whatever the cost, victory or defeat not counting now, they must find water, but find it they didn't because, changing his chant, Mathgen dried up the rivers and streams and lakes and wells of Ireland and there they were, deliriously crossing bogs and climbing mountains, the sound of far away, illusory waterfalls calling them out over precipices to their death.

What the Tuatha Dé Danann didn't yet know was that the chief wizard of the Fomorians could make himself invisible and it was he, altogether more clever than Mathgen, who single-handedly turned what they had already begun to think of as their greatest victory into their greatest defeat, and this he did by going right to the heart of Tuatha Dé Danann country, into a fortress there, and stealing their great harp called Harmonizes Us to All Things.

Next day at the very beginning of their victory celebrations, the Tuatha Dé discovered and suffered their loss.

Putting it to his lips, the chief piper could find no music in his pipe.

Putting it to his lips, the chief trumpeter could find no music in his trumpet.

Putting his bow to it, the chief fiddler could find no music in his fiddle.

Tapping it with his drumstick, the chief drummer could find neither rhythm nor music in his drum.

Opening her mouth, the chief singer could find no music in her voice.

And the curlew didn't call in the bog.

And the blackbird in the willows didn't sing.

Asleep that night on the nine hazel wattles of vision, Mathgen saw what had happened. Macguarch, the chief of Fomorian wizards, had stolen the harp and in stealing that he had stolen the music of Ireland.

That very day, their tongues the colour and shape of cormorant's tongues, the Tuatha Dé were the new Fomorians.

Only Ogma, he being who he was, didn't capitulate to the country-wide epidemic of forgetfulness and brutishness.

Curious about him in the old days, Coirpre the poet had put it to him. 'Which is it?' he asked. 'Is it integrity of being or hadn't brought it back, I wouldn't be asking you this question because mine would be a cormorant's mind, mine would be a cormorant's tongue, and you I'd think of as a man like all others, like myself.'

'As we discovered too late,' Ogma said, 'it was by being able to be invisible that Macguarch stole our music. It was by being able to be visible, all the way out from the ground of my being and their being, that I was able to walk past them bringing it home. Also, I didn't project any obstacles out of myself. I didn't project those monsters and dragons that so often contest the hero's way. There is no part of my mind that I'm not at ease with, that isn't at ease with me.'

So it was that, after all their wars, Fomorians and Tuatha Dé were united by a common question, Ogma.

And now again, harmonized to all things, the Tuatha Dé were of one mind with the wind and the rain. Now again, you could walk through the land and not know they are in it. Yet we, a rougher people who came later to Ireland, out alone in lonely places we will sometimes hear their music. Airs we have heard and, merging our souls with them, we have put out own words to them, calling them 'The Cuilfhionn', 'Caisheal Mumhan', 'Slán Le Maigh', 'Port Na bPucaí', 'Eibhlín a Rún', 'Róisín Dubh' and 'Danny Boy'.

It is why our tongues aren't cormorant tongues. It is why, whatever our history, we can still hear a curlew calling in a bog.

(*Invoking Ireland*, pp. 25–9)

Had he, under tutelage, disciplined the savagery that was in him, and the generosity that was in him, Crunncu might have been a great warrior.

As it turned out, he ended up alone, discovering once to his cost that he hadn't, like his cattle, lost his wildness.

Afterwards, as much as he could, he avoided fairs. And assemblies of his people at Bealtaine and Samhain, and assemblies in honour of Crom Dubh, them also he stayed away from. His four unbroken horses coming down the hillside after her, she came. His door was open.

I'll be a woman to you, she said, going to the fire and putting fresh logs on it. Wild though she was, one of the horses put her head through the door.

Not wishing to give the impression that his house was a stable, or that he lived with his animals, Crunncu went towards her, threatening her.

She didn't move.

The horse and the woman looked at each other.

They looked a long time at each other.

At exactly the same moment, nothing overtly happening between them, the woman turned to her work, the horse backed away, and realizing he was out of his depth, Crunncu asked no questions.

Unsure of himself, he went out.

He stayed out all day, gathering his dry cattle and herding them to higher grazing ground.

The higher view didn't help him.

Heights today didn't mean elevation of thought or of feeling. Being higher than the highest wild goat, being higher than a peregrine falcon bringing wool to her nest, to Crunncu up there looking down on his life's work that meant, not delight, but defeat. Bracken and furze had all but taken over his world. Yet, even now, when last year's bracken was tinder dry, he wouldn't fire it. The fired bracken would fire the furze, but he thought of all that wildness going up in smoke, that was a price he wouldn't pay. Wild nature outside him, letting it be, that was his sacrifice of appeasement to wild nature inside him. Religiously, in ways such as this, Crunncu coped.

Shoulder deep in furze, flowering now, he walked back to his house.

A changed house it was. Nothing had been altered, nothing disturbed, not even the five cobwebs in the five hanging bridles had been molested. And that reassured him. In firelight, now as always, they looked like death masks. Masks of something dead in himself, he sometimes thought.

No, in outward appearance nothing had changed. And yet, particularly at threshold and hearth, it was as if the house had undergone rededication. But to what he didn't know.

Who is she? he wondered, watching her skimming the evening's milk.

Had she come bringing last year's last sheaf of corn, he'd have thought she was the Corn Caillech.

Had she come, walking tall and naked, and holding a spear, he'd have thought she was Scáthach.

Had she come, a lone scaldcrow calling above her, he'd have thought she was Badb Catha.

Had she, having come, opened her thighs and showed her vast vulva, he'd have thought she was Sheela-na-Gig.

Awake, he wondered.

Asleep, he wondered.

Who is she? he wondered, watching her rear like a horse in his dreams.

And the horse that so regularly came to stand in their door? Shoulder deep in the morning, eyes deep in the evening, what did that portend?

There was, he sensed, something he knew about her. But he knew it only where it was safe to know it, in dreamless sleep.

And he wasn't a man to her yet. And in the way that a woman is sometimes a woman to a man, she had so far showed no sign that she wanted to be a woman to him in that welcome way.

And how could any man be a man to a woman like her? How, he looking at her, and she looking at him, could he lay a desiring hand upon her? Would she, showing her teeth, rear like a horse as she did in his dreams?

Sitting across from her by the fire one evening, something dawned on him: Until she came his house had sheltered him, but only as a shed might shelter a cow. Like a religion now, it sheltered him inwardly. Like a religion that was there from the beginning, like a religion that had grown with the growing world, it sheltered him in his difficult depths.

It was strange.

> A horse, and she not broken, standing shoulder deep
> In his door every morning
> A horse, and she not broken, standing hip deep
> In his door every evening.

From hip deep in his nature the dream came: walking high moors he was when he came upon it, the tall standing stone. Taller than a man, it was a man's member, or a god's member, and it was suffering. As a woman in labour suffers, it was suffering. And then, up from the roots a shuddering came, upwards it shuddered, upwards it surged into a long releasing scream that awakened Crunncu, and lying there he knew that in some strange way he had been a man to the woman who was lying beside him.

Welcome to the great world, she said.

Terror of what had happened was shaking Crunncu.

Till dawn it continued, shaking the shaken foundations of old established mind in him, of old established mood in him.

I'm ruined, he said.

Walk through the ruins, she said.

Walk through the ruins you've already walked through.

Walk in the great world you've already walked into.

It's a nothing, a nowhere, I've walked into, he said.

No more marvellous place than that nothing, that nowhere, she said. It's God, she said. It's the Divine behind God, behind all gods, she said. It's the Divine out of which the gods and the stars are born, she said.

My name is Macha, she said.

For the first time since waking Crunncu opened his eyes, opened them in anger, in dangerous, frightened anger.

We should never call anyone Macha but Macha, he blazed.

Do you hear me? We should never call anyone Macha but Macha.

Macha's name is a holy name. It belongs to no one but Macha. To no one, no one. To no one but Macha.

His anger became religious indignation, he fixed her in a cold stare: your name isn't Macha! In this house it isn't Macha. I keep horses for Macha. In honour of Macha, in praise of Macha, in thanksgiving to Macha, I never, not even in a moment of greed, I never attempt to bridle them, I never attempt to break them in. Wild on the hills, neighing on the hills, their manes and their tails streaming in the hills, they are the glory of Macha. They are the nearest we can ever come, safely come, to a vision of Macha.

    In her nature Macha
    In her name Macha
  Sharing neither nature nor name with anyone, that is Macha.

Taking Macha's name you have sinned against Macha. Taking Macha's name you aren't safe to sit with, you aren't safe to eat with, you aren't safe to live with, to lie with. What I cannot understand is why our cow hasn't run dry, is why our well hasn't run dry. In my house, no! In my house your name is not Macha.

By what name then shall I be known?

By the name of my neighbour's nag.

What's her name?

She has no name. Nag is her name. And it's your name. Until you find favour with Macha, it is your name. Nag is your name! Nag!

And how might that be? How might I find favour with Macha?

That's for Macha to decide. She might never decide. Macha's heart can be hoof hard. And her head! No! Macha's holy head has never been bridled. Cobwebs blind the bridles we would bridle Macha with. The bridles we would bridle Macha with are masks of our own terror. Attempt to bridle Macha as you'd attempt to bridle an ordinary horse, attempt it, just that, and your face will fall in, into nothingness, into emptiness, into your own empty skull looking back at you as the bridle you'd have bridled her with.

A HUT AT THE EDGE OF THE VILLAGE

Macha is lovely Macha is ugly

Macha is gentle Macha is vicious

Macha has arms Macha has hooves

The most beautiful of women is Macha: she opens her thighs and you see a mare's mouth.

Macha is Life
Macha is Death

Bigger life than the life we live is Macha
Bigger death than the death we die is Macha

With no ritual have we bridled Macha.
With no religion have we broken her in.
In no temple to Macha have we stabled Macha.

Everything in the world that we aren't able for, that's Macha.
Everything in ourselves that we aren't able for, that's Macha.
Everything religion isn't able for, everything culture isn't able for,
That's Macha.

Stories we have that can cope with Crom Dubh.
No story we have or ever will have can cope with Macha.

Search our stories, our Tains and Toraiochts, and in them you'll find not a hoof-mark of Macha, in them you'll find not a shake of her tail.
No! No! Neither Tain nor Toraiocht has covered Macha. Rising on its hind legs like a stallion, our Aill at Uisnech hasn't covered Macha.
Living in a world as wild as this one is, the only goddess or god I leave a door open for, and leave a fire on for, is a goddess or god who hasn't

submitted to our sanctimonies and sacraments, who hasn't submitted to religion. And that's Macha.

> For Macha I leave my door open.
> For Macha I leave my fire lighting at night.

> Macha hasn't been covered by culture.
> Macha hasn't been covered by religion.

Who or what could cover Macha? he asked.
You have covered Macha, she replied.
Outraged and afraid, he was on the floor pulling on his clothes and his boots.
Hearing her walk away, he looked up.
Hearing hooves on the yard, he went to the door.
It was May morning and Crunncu knew, too late he knew, that it wasn't his neighbour's nag who neighed from the hills.

(Dreamtime, pp. 13–17)

It is a story soon told. Art was king in Tara, a hill from which on a clear day he could see his entire kingdom. It was foreshown to him that in a battle soon to be fought in the far west he would be killed by Lughaidh mac Con, a pretender to the throne. On the night before the battle he lay with Achtan the daughter of a famous druid. In time Achtan gave birth to a boy child. Calling him Cormac mac Airt, the druid his grandfather chanted five protective circles about him, against wounding, drowning, fire, sorcery and wolves. Knowing that Lughaidh intended their destruction, Achtan sought refuge for herself and Cormac in a trackless wilderness. As they slept together one night on a bed of leaves a milch wolf came and stole the child. Taking him to her cave in Keshcorran, she suckled him, he drinking her two middle tits as dry as her five cubs drank theirs dry.

Months later a hunter climbed towards the Keshcorran caves. He saw the child playing with the wolves. Guessing who he was, he waited till the whole pack had gone off on the hunt and then he rescued him, taking him to Achtan.

Knowing how soon Lughaidh would be on the prowl, Achtan decided to seek refuge with Fiachna Casán in Ulster. Fiachna was Art's foster father. As she crossed a mountain at night the wolves of Ireland came from far and near seeking the child, claiming him as theirs. Surrounding them, a herd of wild horses escorted mother and child all the way to safety in Fiachna's house.

One day, a young man now, Cormac set out for Tara. Keeping the hill to his right, he came upon a woman in dishevelled distress. Enquiring the cause, she told him that her sheep had grazed the queen's woad field in the night and now they were forfeit to her.

'A shearing for a shearing, the wool for the woad, that would have been more just,' Cormac said.

Within hours the judgment was famous, known by everyone, except the king, in Tara.

When he did hear of it, Lughaidh knew that the one who delivered it was the rightful heir to the throne. Defeated in a way that he couldn't be in battle, he resigned and soon preparations were underway for Cormac's inauguration.

No small matter this. Not something for one morning only.

First, in a manner most sacred, he must marry Meadhbh, the goddess of sovereignty. Meadhbh was dangerous and strange. Could be, you would look at her and she would be the ugliest and foulest thing you could imagine. Turning away in utter, sickening revulsion you would for some reason be tempted to look back and now she would be fair beyond anything you could imagine. The one who was destined to be king must be able to lie with her foul and fair.

There was a king's chariot at Tara. Yoked to it were two horses of the same colour, horses that had never been harnessed. Wilder than the wildest horse, the chariot would rear up and throw off someone who wasn't true enough and just enough and wise enough to be king.

There were at Tara two thunderous standing stones called Blocc and Bluigne, with only a hand's breadth between them. They too must accept the one who would be king, opening before his chariot horses, letting him ride regally through.

There is in Tara a standing, stone phallus called Fál. The one who would be king must ride past it and if, as he does so, it doesn't screech against his chariot axle, he is rejected.

Cormac lay with Meadhbh, the goddess of sovereignty, fair and foul.

Stepping up into it, the royal chariot didn't rear up and throw him off.

The purple mantle on the prow of the chariot fitted him perfectly.

The two thunderous standing stones, Blocc and Bluigne, opened before his chariot horses, letting him ride regally through.

Riding past it, Fál, the stone phallus, screeched against his chariot axle.

On the morrow, Cormac, who had been suckled by a wolf, was crowned king.

Never before or since was there a reign like it in Ireland.

More than swineherds could dream of or imagine, there was beech mast and acorns in the woods. Salmon and sea trout ran in the rivers. Cattle were as lovely to look at in March as they were coming down from high grazing ground in October. The calls of grouse calling in the mountains were as bright as their combs. No warrior came home with the heads of his enemies hanging from the manes of his chariot horses. No druid chanted a killing or a maddening incantation. People died as they lived, at ease with a world they had flourished in. And all of this because of Fír Flathemon, the wisdom and truth and justice of the ruler.

That, in little, is the story.

Before anything else, perhaps, what we notice is how etymologically clamant it is. Art means Bear. Lughaidh mac Con means Lughaidh son of Wolf. And Cormac mac Airt means Cormac son of Bear. What we have therefore is dynastic interruption and restoration, Wolf defeating Bear in battle and Bear defeating Wolf in wisdom. Wisdom specifically in the determination and exercise of justice.

Only it isn't so exogamously simple. Between the usurpation and the restoration Wolf suckles the child who is Boy and Bear, gives her life-milk to the child who is Boy and Bear, and so it is that, in this stolen child, Boy and Bear and Wolf are foster brothers.

In the unalarmed language of legend, Cormac who is the son of a human father and mother is also a son of Bear and a son of Wolf. In a world that is still able for such things, Cormac mac Airt is Cormac mac Con in flight from Lughaidh mac Con. The child who is Boy and Bear and Wolf in flight from Wolf.

Etymologically, at this point, the story seems to be saying that at birth we are a multiplicity of shape-shifting possibilities, not an essentially unalterable unity.

In identification with Cormac, we ask who are we, and the answer is troubling.

And now a night like no other, ever, in Ireland – the wolves of Ireland, all of them, no matter where, throw back their heads and howl unanimously, and then, coming in long, lonesome strides, they surround the fleeing mother and child, claiming him as Wolf Son, their son.

The question now is: fenced ever more narrowly in by it, can we emerge from nature into culture? Can we emerge from wolfish ways into what we fondly think of as human, humane ways?

Extraordinarily, it is with the help of a herd of wild horses that we do so. Breaking through the snarling claim of nature to us, they walk with us to Fiachna's door, he a renowned druid and teacher.

How did Cormac take to culture?

Did he wolfishly reject it?

When being wolfish wasn't enough in getting his own way, would he suddenly turn bearish?

Even when he began to be more human than animal would the wolf in him suddenly steal him back into his wolfish werewolfish ways, would the bear in him suddenly steal him back into his bearish, berserk ways?

In emotion and mood was he subject to sudden and spontaneous shapeshift?

Was it, at best, that a thin crust of human ways came to overlay his deeper and more abiding wolfish ways?

Or, all teaching and talk having failed, did he one day come thunderstruck down from the hills, wild nature and druidic culture singing a perfectly single song in him?

Noticing it, did neighbours come round to the difficult idea that the lightning had a hand in his reconstruction, in his refinement?

Finally, did they come round to the yet more difficult idea that deep within him, explaining his brightness, a diamond had formed?

Could he, in the light of that diamond, see into all worlds, into all causes of all things?

We do not know.

Having the silences and imaginative omissions of a folktale or a ballad, the story only tells us that, coming to him one morning, Fiachna said, 'Today is a good day to go south and assume kingship in Tara.'

Etymologically self-assured, he did go south.

And now again, Blocc and Bluigne opened before us.

Now again, announcing Fír Flathemon in Ireland, Fál, the stone phallus, screeched.

AFTERTHOUGHTS

Carry the lad that's born to be king over lands and lakes, over bogs and through woods, to fosterage with a druid in Ulster.

The lad who has a milch wolf for a foster mother and a druid for a foster father.

The lad who undergoes fosterage in nature before he undergoes fosterage in culture, in druidic culture.

The lad who must ever afterwards know the equal claims upon him of nature and of culture.

The lad who in virtue of natural descent from his natural father is Cormac mac Airt, is Cormac son of Bear, and who in virtue of fosterage to a wolf-mother is Cormac mac Con, is Cormac son of Wolf.

This lad who was born to be king and who became king, did he, in heraldry flying from standard and pole and rampart-wall, declare himself to be a march-man, a man of the marches, of the march-lands, between animal and human?

Given his lineage natural and cultural, how secure in any particular identity could Cormac be? In his deepest, unremembered dreams, did he migrate among identities? Awake, would he sometimes be seized by dread of turning into a bear, by dread of turning into a wolf, by dread of becoming a were-bear, a were-wolf?

Did Cormac fear battle, thinking that in charge after charge, and blow by blow, a blind fury would build in him, and he would become a berserker?

Insecure in his identity, did Cormac ever dream that his purple, royal robe had become a bear-sack, a bear-shirt, a bear-coat? The bear-shirt, the bear-coat of a berserk?

In older times, when someone wished to become a were-wolf, he would anoint his whole body in magical oils and he would wear a girdle made of wolf-skin. Did Cormac ever dream that his wolf-mother came to him with such a girdle? To meet her on her terms was he tempted to turn wolf, to become werewolf?

The story of this lad who is born to be king builds to a supreme crisis when, claiming him for nature, the wolves of Ireland close in on him, close in on a fugitive mother and child. Intermediaries between nature and culture, their kind co-operating in culture with humanity, a herd of wild horses break through the wolf-circle, the wolf-girdle, and escort both mother and child back into culture. Does this mean that, claimed by culture, he is now lost to nature?

Or, fostered by both, did Cormac emerge as a perfect unanimity of nature and culture in a single, supremely assured, sovereign identity, a king before he was king by copulation with Meadhbh, the goddess of sovereignty.

And this perfect unanimity of wild nature and druidic culture in him – that, surely, was the source of Fír Flathemon in him.

Wolf's milk, the milk of wild nature, that and the nurturing graces of druidic incantation and ritual gave to Cormac a distinction at once natural and cultured, at once animal and heraldic.

Recognizing the perfect unanimity of wild nature and druidic culture in Cormac mac Airt, in Cormac mac Con, the newly yoked horses at Tara didn't leap at him, Blocc and Bluigne opened before him and, as he rode past it, Fál, the stone phallus, screeched against his chariot axle.

Heard throughout the land, it was the screech of fertility in nature and culture.

(*Invoking Ireland*, pp. 46–52)

I No Longer Smelled of Thunder
— *On Ecology* —

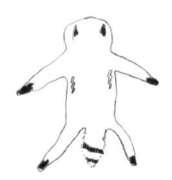

In the epic of Gilgamesh, when Enkidu the wild man rises from his lovemaking the animals flee from him. Eden is over. Seemingly without choice, he walks into the bright walls of the city and everything changes. We all feel the loss of that. Without archiving the moment to a scene from a tablet, Moriarty throws us like clay to be forged in the struggle between committee and mystic, innocence and experience. There we are, men and women, caught in the wrestle between Gilgamesh and Enkidu. The village and the forest.

The ecology Moriarty evokes is not exactly a nostalgia for drinking with the antelope at the waterhole (though a casual glance could imply it), it is for the integrity of the wrestle. Between high street and sweat lodge, strip club and Uluru. He's not a prude, or a flat-Earth evangelical.

But John is right to push for the sanctity of wild, divine intelligence.

Because maybe the wrestle was rigged.

Maybe it was a done deal the moment the Hairy Man walked through the gates. It wasn't an even playing field. Because it appears Gilgamesh won, that Hadrian's wall was erected, Alexander struck his blade through the Gordian knot.

And our relationship to the wild is no longer a wrestle, it's an execution.

In this flash of writings we witness Moriarty's sheer naturalness to the ecological world. Nothing is unpacked to the point of tedium, you are simply left with the possibility that John is having the barley, peregrine or raindrop almost speak through him in a way that humans – tone-deaf as we mostly are these days – could possibly comprehend.

That's not meant as an inflation, simply that there seems to be some cross-species gossip going on. Moriartian ecology frees us from the gridiron of green statistics, the naivety of the New Age, and most of all, keeps some door open to the miraculous. Delight replaces grim-faced obligation.

This selection makes no attempt
To achieve a holistic calm,
Or generalized sentiment,
It should,
As John would wish,
Anoint us in horse piss.

This I believed: there are two ways we could have gone, the way of the Titan, Prometheus, or the way of the dolphin. In the Promethean way we shape nature to suit us, in the way of the dolphin we let nature shape us to suit it. Everywhere there is evidence that we have chosen wrongly.

No doubt about it, though, in doing what I was doing I was Promethean. On four days a week in three different gardens I was shaping nature, and to see the difference my efforts were making I only had to walk on to some fallow bog beyond the trees in Lisnabrucka or, the next day, beyond the trees in Leitirdyfe. The compromise was, to live as though it mattered to not make too much noise in the world and to continue surrendered to nature in places deeper within me than my grip on scythe or spade, than my grip on myself.

Often in my case, of course, there would be reservation and second thoughts in the surrender.

I saw genius everywhere I looked in nature, but that didn't mean that it was everywhere benign.

I would remember a day in Inishbofin when I went superficially to sea in their fishing boat with James Coyne and Stephen Lavelle and Ned Burke. That first lobster pot they hauled from the seabed – what a zoo of hissing, snapping, seething life it was, the crabs and the lobster foaming and bubbling atrocity and massacre from their small mouths and the crabs with their pink claws and the lobster with his blue claws snapping at air, but it could be at the galaxy or it could be at God they were snapping, and the conger eel, his back and flanks dark grey, his belly pale, he going furiously round and round at the bottom of the pot and seeking to extrude from within himself a new sea of slime to swim in, and a sea slug dressed in a patchwork, in a bluff, of poisons, green, purple and blue. Knife at the ready, his eyes as alert as gannet's eyes, James advances his hand down into all this ostentatious deadliness and, faster than life on the sea floor, he severs the eel's head, or almost. It is still hanging on by the skin of its throat. Hauling him out, slippery with slime though he is, James slashes the coupling skin, he heaves the headless body into the sea and reflexively there at our feet on the deck, the wide-eyed head snaps, snaps, snaps, snaps. Expertly, indeed with exquisite skill, he handles the crabs out through the hatch, he breaks off the claws, throws them into a bucket, and throws the not so pleasantly edible remainder into the sea. The starfish and the sea slug are easy to deal with. The lobster is preserved whole, to be boiled alive and whole, and to be then served up with cordon bleu good manners to a gourmet in a Paris restaurant.

One lobster pot hauled and cleared. Seventy-nine to go.

For me, that day, that first lobster pot was the dot at the bottom of a question mark set up alongside the universe we live in. Is ours an utterly deviant planet? Or is the hauled lobster pot the astronomical norm? If it is in fact the norm then to continue surrendered to nature in the hope that it will shape me to suit it mightn't be the wisest of moves. Already, after all, in both instinct and dentition, it has shaped me to meat-eating, and that I resist. On the increasingly shaky assumption that they do seek their wellbeing exclusively in nature, could it be that dolphins also have some thinking to do?

The hauled lobster pot is the dot in the question mark questioning anthropus:

?

Three thousand miles over the ocean from where we fished that day, in an entrance to what we call the New World, Lady Liberty holds her torch aloft. This, perhaps the great gesture of the modern Western world, would be more trustworthy, surely it would, I thought, cycling one morning to work, if, in sculptural rhythm with it, she held the living lobster pot in her other hand, that a hanging hand holding what we must some day come to think of as our inner phylogenetic ancient regime. This it was that took over and ran the French and Russian revolutions into reigns of terror. But what was I doing, still arguing like this with myself? Our eighteenth-century meliorist bluff minotaurically called in me, I had long ago concluded that our best way into a New World was to ascend the Colorado into the Canyon and all the way up along Bright Angel Trail.

(*Curlew*, pp. 16–17)

Here in Kerry I live among mountains, some of them almost touchably near, all of them breaking and raising my horizon, higher than the highest-flying ravens by day, high as high-hunting Orion at night. And these mountains, all of them, have old names, the Paps, Croghane, Bennaun Mór, Stoompa, the Blind Horse's Glen with its three lakes and its almost perpendicular back wall, Mangerton Mountain, Torc Mountain and, not entirely eclipsing the Reeks, a cluster of Bens called

Toomies. Northwards, the world stretches away across the hilly, rolling lands of north Kerry and west Limerick.

To live in a place so heartbreakingly beautiful can be a difficult blessing. Sooner or later as I'd sit here writing in the morning I would lift my head and look out and, as arrestingly as a heart attack or a stroke, what I'd see would invalidate me in my opinions and purposes.

Here, in such a world on such a day, opinions and purposes are a Fall or at the very least they are the agents and symptoms of our exile from what we paradisaically are at the core of our being.

There at the core of our being we are as pure as a drop of water on a lotus leaf.

Two things are unassailably and irreconcilably true on such a day: perceived with clear eyes, with eyes naked of preconception, reality as a whole is immaculate, is perfect, is pure, that even though three stone-fenced fields away a fox is plundering a wren's nest and is ravenously killing and devouring the still bald chicks, they themselves, every time their mother returns with her mouth full of death, seeming to be little more than luridly shrieking voracities for insects and grubs.

To survive at all on such a day I'd have to forgo being a self: where normally I would say 'I see,' now in self-abeyance I would say 'seeing is'.

On such a day it is good to know and still better it is to act on the knowledge that the subjective-objective divide is a dispensable piece of mental machinery, the mechanism of our alienation, turning us into spectators.

The fourteenth way of looking at a blackbird or at Torc Mountain is to remove the one who looks from the looking.

Blake tells us that 'the Eye altering alters all'.

It is in altering itself philosophically that the eye alters itself optically.

In a dream I am standing at the side of a secondary road, hitchhiking home. It turns out to be a long wait. It is already nightfall when a car comes along. I am not at all surprised to see Bishop Berkeley at the wheel. 'No,' he says, 'I cannot take you all the way but I can take you as far as a village called Esse Est Percipi.' 'Is there a round tower in that village?' I ask. 'Yes, there is,' he says, So far so good, I think. I am happy to get in. And now I notice that his canonical cap, certainly in colour and shape, is an amanita muscaria mushroom.

And there is a story I tell myself. I hear a knock on my door in the night. Who can it be, I wonder, at this late hour? Expecting bad news, I go and open it. Orion, a Siderius Nuncius reduced to our size, is standing there. Handing me a packet, he tells me that in it is everything that human beings have thought about the universe. The universe doesn't recognize itself in any of it. It has delegated me to return it. Almost instantly, reassuming stellar size, he is back up there brightening the sky above Mangerton Mountain.

It is something that happens to me again and again: lifting my head, I look out and all the concepts with which I seek to understand reality come home empty-handed to me. And what a blessedness that is: to be languageless before reality.

As Wallace Stevens has it, 'The plum survives its poems.'

So violably beautiful some days is Torc Mountain that it would already be huge hurt to it and to me were I to seek to do anything other than to selflessly and passively perceive it. On such days if I had no sense of soul in myself it would be soul to me.

We remember our great subversives, Yajnavalkya, the Buddha, Lao Tzu and Jesus. If you find them tough going, then come and experience an even bigger challenge to all your preconceptions, come and stand before Torc Mountain.

Of two mountains, Torc Mountain and Mount Sinai, the thunders and the lightnings and the supernatural terrors of smoking, quaking Mount Sinai threaten me far less in my personal integrity than does the wholly natural, unnecessary beauty of Torc.

Torc could be ugly and still exist.

The world could be utterly ugly and still exist.

So how come a world that as well as existing, is also beautiful? Is tremendous? Is stupendous in daisy and galaxy?

Rilke is on to something when he says that beauty is the beginning of terror that we are just about able to bear.

'O what can ail thee, knight-at-arms,
    Alone and palely loitering?
The sedge has withered from the lake,
    And no birds sing.'

The knight's answer might be, I stood before Torc Mountain on a day when, revealing it and concealing it, draperies of mist and wholly occluding banks of mist were coming and going upon it.

'And this is why I sojourn here
    Alone and palely loitering,
Though the sedge is withered from the lake,
    And no birds sing.'

That is how dangerous beauty is to the purposes and opinions around which we have constituted ourselves.

And what a destiny, to find myself living in front of Torc Mountain, with the setting Sun burning in winter in the gap between it and Mangerton and burning in spring in the gap between it and Toomies.

Unlike the Paps, whose nipples are tombs; unlike Slieve Mish, which is home to a god in whom Ireland is ultimate not just geographically; unlike the Reeks, with their Hag's Glen and their Devil's Ladder and their Heavenly Gates; unlike the mountains of Uíbh Rathach, among them a high pass, a gap between worlds, called Bealach Oisín; unlike Scelec, whose winding stair ascends from plaice to Pisces and yet higher, from crab to Cancer and yet higher – unlike these, Torc is both mythless and legendless, and the boar it is associated by name with, he too is mythless and legendless.

I think of St Patrick and Oisín, the Christian and the pagan: coming to Torc in the course of their memorial wanderings around Ireland, Patrick exclaims, At last! At last! A dind with no shenchus attached to it. A thing, a big blue thing, not claimed by our cultural past, a thing, a big blue thing, not eclipsed by our thinking about it!

I daily experience his surprise and joy. To stand before Torc is eureka. And challenge. Big and blue on my south-western horizon, it is an invitation to pure perceiving and, at whatever cost to our habitual sense of ourselves, in pure perceiving is huge salvation.

At odds with Greek myth in this, at odds indeed with his mother in this, I some days look at Torc and I dare to believe that, if I can, then so can the Minotaur experience himself as Miranda.

In Connemara, on a day when there wasn't much to me, the Owenmore river was my external guarantee that there is soul in the world and soul in me. Here it is Torc.

Torc and the Owenmore: knowing them I do not need to find a hearing with angels, not as Rilke did.

On its day, seen not just from where I live, Torc is an invitation to another history than the one we are so sadly and so uncreatively bogged down in.

What Mount Sinai is to Jews Torc can be to us, the mountain before which we will re-experience and reimagine ourselves, a people living from the pure blue soul, from the Torc-blue soul, that we have in common with the world.

By soul I do not mean something metaphysical. By soul I mean what seeing is when we look at Torc or what hearing is when, out of doors in a sightless night, we listen to the roar of the Abha Garbh, become monotone over distance, as it tumbles through a ravine that hangs down the mountainside from the Horse's Glen.

Also not claimed by local lore, yet looking very much like local lore, are the thorns that grow within the ravine. They rise from among boulders that seem unshiftable yet have been shifted. The high lakes of the Horse's Glen and two days of rain behind it, the big, roaring rush of water has done the impossible. It is up from among these dense, mineral immensities, tumbled as they are about the place, that the thorns grow. I inhale the not entirely pleasant fragrance of their flowers in May and I eat their haws in October, and always the one thing and the other makes me feel strange to myself. It's as if I had taken an utterly esoteric, an utterly countercultural, way of seeing and knowing into myself. Days later, I will still have no mind to talk about the things that people talk about. And for now I am sure that there is another than the scientific way of knowing the universe. For now I know that there is another than the scientific way of knowing the mind that would know atoms and stars.

(*Curlew,* pp. 297–300)

I imagine that I am standing on the moon. I look at Earthrise and instantly I know that to properly greet it I must let Mesopotamia, Egypt, Judaea, Greece and Rome fall out of my eyes and mind. I must let Europe fall out of how I see and know things. What I also know is that in the course of time there will be much that I will pick up, but for now I must endure what I am enduring, the terror and exhilaration of a perception minimally modified by conception. So silently marvellous is the perception, is the sensation, that modifying mind cannot find entry.

Soon it does find entry and concepts that come upon and cover the sensation, that translucently cover it, are oriental.

First I think that the wonder I am looking at is padmasambhava, is lotus born.

The lotus has its roots in the mud at the bottom of a pool or lake. In its stem it rises up through the water, spreading its flat green pads for support on the surface of the water, it efflores to the Sun. Immemorially in India this marvel of natural ascent has been seen as an analogue of spiritual ascent. Having our roots in the mud of the passions, we rise up through the brightening water and then secure on the surface we open out to divine irradiation.

To be lotus born is to be born into what we are in utmost efflored transcendence.

Looking at the Earth from the moon, the only conception that suits the perception is padmasambhava. The Earth I am looking at is lotus born.

Going further, the sensation demanding it, I find myself saying that the Earth I am looking at is ratnasambhava, it is gem born, jewel born, born not just of the lotus but of the jewel at the heart of the lotus.

> The Earth
> > seen from the Moon.

Tell me that its subatomic particles are hosannas and I will say, Yes, looking at it, that I believe.

Tell me that its subatomic particles are the quavers and the demiquavers of an oratorio too supernal for angels and I will say, Yes, looking at it, that I believe.

Hard it is, looking at it, to believe that time was when Tyrannosaurus was rex in it.

Hard to believe that the hammerhead shark is a perfection of morally qualmless life in it.

Hard to credit the Colosseumed red roar that rises up out of it, all the way up among the intelligent stars.

Hard to credit the whistlings of nacht-und-nebel trains rising ad astra out of it.

Hard to believe what Christians believe, that the God who they say created it had to go down into it to Harrow its Hells.

And yet, just look at how it looks from the Moon.

I think of Lorenzo and Jessica in *The Merchant of Venice*:

> Sit, Jessica: look, how the floor of heaven
> Is thick inlaid with patines of bright gold:
> There's not the smallest orb which thou behold'st
> But in his motion like an angel sings
> Still quiring to the young-eyed cherubims;
> Such harmony is in immortal souls;
> But, whilst this muddy vesture of decay
> Doth grossly close it in, we cannot hear it.

Seen coming over a lunar horizon, the Earth itself is surely such an orb. Surely it is what Milton would call a crystall sphear:

> Ring out, ye crystall sphears,
> Once bless our human ears
> > (If ye have power to touch our senses so)

> And let your silver chime
> Move in melodious time
> > And let the base of heaven's deep organ blow
> And with your ninefold harmony
> Make up full consort to th' Angelike symphony.
> For if such holy song
> Enwrap our fancy long,
> > Time will run back, and fetch the age of gold,
> And speck'ld vanity
> Will sicken soon and die,
> > And leprous sin will melt from earthly mould,
> And hell itself will pass away
> And leave her dolorous mansions to the peering day.

Tell me, as I lunarly look at it, that the Earth is a crystall note in a silver chime and I will say Yes, that it is.

The crystall note.
The Colosseumed red roar.

The silver chime.
Two bull tyrannosaurs growling screechily at each other.

I imagine a people much like ourselves indigenous to the Moon.
    Just think of what a lunar Lorenzo would say to a lunar Jessica as they watched the wonder climbing into their night sky.
    Just think of what a lunar Milton seeing it would say.
    Just think of how our quiring orb, our crystall sphear, would figure in their myths.
    How would a lunar Elgar hear it?
    What would they think watching an asteroid crash into it?
    What would it astrologically mean to them to be born under an ascendent Earth?
    In what way or ways would their medicine men and medicine women draw down the power of the Earth?

Would they stand under it in the way that Akenaten and Nefertiti used to stand under the divine Egyptian Sun, its beams turning into hands to accept their daily offerings?

I imagine it, a lunar people greeting Earthrise as Ancient Egygptians greeted Sunrise.

I imagine it, a lunar Book of the Dead speaking for a lunar Ani:

O Earth-orb, Lord of the Earth-beams, who shines forth from the horizon every day: may you shine in the face of Ani, for he worships you in the morning, he propitiates you in the evening. May the soul of Ani go up with you to the sky, may he travel in the day-bark, may he moor in the night- bark, may he mix with the unwearying stars in the sky.

I imagine them, lunar baboons facing Earthrise.

We have faced Earthrise.

That takes getting used to.

Attempting to take it in, I say it again:

We have faced Earthrise.

And the challenge to us now is, how can we turn what is so far a historical moment into an evolutionary moment?

The Christian answer is already to hand: consciously and recuperatively pioneered by Jesus, Bright Angel Trail has become the Triduum Sacrum Trail and, at the wholly mystical end of it, there it is, the Earth coming over its own karmic horizon,

there it is,

Earthrise.

A HUT AT THE EDGE OF THE VILLAGE

*

In the absence of a grand and essential as opposed to a tangential challenge we corrupt. To verify this we only have to walk in any street of any modern city anywhere in the world.

Hebrew wisdom has it that where there is no vision the people perish.

Egyptians learned to journey through the underworld with the Sun. They learned to journey through to sunrise and to an afterlife among the unwearying stars with the Sun. Alternatively, taking to the underworld path pioneered and kept open by the Sun, they learned how to journey to Sekhet-Aaru.

A most serious reservation for the moment allayed, this we must admit was and is one of the great human audacities. The question is: in the way that Egyptians journeyed with the Sun to sunrise are we willing, in acceptance of a common destiny with it, to journey with the Earth to Earthrise?

Almost always, for better or for worse, our humanity is as much a cultural acquirement as it is something naturally given to us and surely that is why we should settle for nothing less than a great culture, great in that it proposes and provides for great purposes and goals. Earthrise is a great goal and in being willing to participate in it we would at the very least be laying ourselves open to the possibility of greatness in our humanity. Also, in this we would be showing ourselves willing to symbiose our frightened, fleeing histories with final evolutionary transitions already realized but awaiting cultural selection.

Astonishingly, what we need to select is Bright Angel Trail. Having in all its strata undergone immense mutations in Christ, Bright Angel Trail is now the Triduum Sacrum Trail. In architectural and ritual transposition, it is the religious road home.

(*Night Journey*, pp. 257–60)

There is a Gaelic poem of the fifteenth century called 'A Luin Doire an Chairn', in English 'The Blackbird of Derrycairn'.

Anticipating Marvell and Yeats in this, it is, in an initially insecure sense of it, 'A Dialogue of Self and Soul', that even though it exhibits itself as a monologue, Self in this case having not just all the good lines; Self, as in a world where the winner takes all, having the only overt voice. Being agonistic however, that voice inevitably conjures and gives leave to the other, even if only as articulate silence.

Esoteric to the poem is an old story:

The land bright in hill and lake with legends of his father, his mother a hind of the highlands, Oisín could be a stag in the woods or a warrior at your side and if, in the battle with the King of the World, he was at your side, no harm would come to you, and that evening sitting by a fire of hazel stumps and faggots, his bones as beautiful as his mother's, his eyes as alert and timid, he would be a poet, crying right there as the eagle of Glen na bFuath does, whistling as the otters of Drom Dhá Loch do, and crowing as the grouse of Cruachán Chuinn do.

A morning in May it was, by Loch Leane in the south-west, Oisín saw her, a woman not of our world, nor of any world that could neighbour our world, so entirely lovely was she as she came riding towards him over the brightened lake and along the brightened shore.

Greeting him, she invited him to ride with her to her land, perfect and blessed she said it was, and in the mountains in the south-west, there is a pass and to this day it is called Bealach Oisín, the pass or gap through which, riding behind her on her white horse, Oisín rode with Niamh Cinn Óir to the Land of the Ever Young.

Even though in that blessed land it only felt like three days, as time is with us Oisín was gone for three hundred years.

Eventful years they were. Eventful first and foremost because St Patrick came ashore and, the great pagan druids no match for him in learning and in magic, he founded the new Christian order converting kings and chieftains and peasants and serfs wherever he went.

A HUT AT THE EDGE OF THE VILLAGE

Also, as the story has it, it was during these years that we human beings lapsed to our present, greatly diminished stature and strength.

Riding back into Ireland after what for him was so short an absence, Oisín had a hard time of it getting used to so much unhappy alteration in people and things.

As he rode, sad at heart, across this once mighty and marvellous land in which your mother could be a hind and your father so out of the ordinary that our oldest folktales, silent a long time, again lived out their wonders and dangers and horrors and marvels in him, riding slack reined, not caring where, he came upon three diminished men attempting but failing to lift a boulder. Bending sideways down, he put his mighty hand, his hand of the old days, under it, but, as he lifted it, his saddle girth snapped, down he came, and that was it, full bodily contact with the diminished Earth diminished him.

What the story doesn't say but what we can say is that the diminished Earth is its reflection back to us of our diminished view of it. In itself it is as tremendous and folkloric and as instinct with wonder and terror as it ever was.

And what is true of the Earth is true also of ourselves.

It is to diminished seeing and knowing that we and the world have together fallen victim.

Were we to outgrow this diminishment, we would once again have need of tales altogether taller and altogether deeper than current common sense.

But, as ever, that's an old story doing and saying new things in the new telling.

Returning to its original, simple self, it sets the scene for the poem before us.

In that poem, catching us unawares as it were, catching us before we have time to compose ourselves to reluctance or reception, Oisín, the revenant from the pagan world, has already engaged our attention and here we are listening with him to a blackbird singing beside her nest. What is more, his listening and therefore our listening is lauds:

> *Binn sin, a luin Doire an Chairn*
> *ní chuala mé in aird sa bhith*
> *Ceol ba binne ná do cheol*
> *agus tú fá bhun do nid.*

An indication not a translation: lovely it is, lovely and sweet your song, blackbird of Derrycairn. Never in the world or in any height of the world have I heard such mellow quavers coming from a bill so yellow. The honey of generation breaking into the black and yellow andantes of your song it is, the whole song as perfect as the perfect bowl and rim of your nest.

And so, breaking briefly off from his natural lauds in and of the natural world, Oisín having turned and talked to the bird now turns and talks to St Patrick:

> *Aoincheol is binne fán mbith,*
>
> > *mairg nach éisteann leis go fóil,*
> > *a mhic Calprainn na gclog mbínn*
> > *'s go mbéartha arís ar do nóin.*

In other words: Sad it is that you, St Patrick, will not listen to the bird, more especially since, having listened, you could go back into ascetic, cold claustration and continue from where you left off, chanting your nones.

Here we are then, in the toils of an agon between the blackbird and the bell, between the blackbird who invites us to immanence and the bell, St Patrick's bronze bell newly heard in Ireland, that summons us to transcendence.

And here it is, on a second or third reading of the poem, that we begin to have doubts about our initial estimation of it as A Dialogue of Body and Soul or as A Dialogue of Self and Soul.

Pagan that he is, Oisín is not talking to us out of a preconceived or most of all out of an experienced dualism of Body and Soul or of Self and Soul. Likely it is that, had he to openly argue the thing with Patrick, he would propose that our mortality is at once both a wonderfully and dreadfully enriching way for us to experience our immortality. Instead, therefore, of the blackbird or the bell, the blackbird and the bell. If only he will come out and listen to the blackbird, Oisín is unreservedly happy to see St Patrick going back into claustration there to continue laying himself ascetically open to transcendence, or to what Patrick, given leave to speak, would almost surely call the adventure, the sometimes tremendous adventure, of life lived sacramentally in and towards Transcendence.

A man of the out-of-doors that otter and eagle hunt in and that red-combed grouse crow in, Oisín now tells us that it isn't to any ordinary blackbird that we are listening. Presumably because of an unusual sweetness in his singing, Fionn mac Cumhaill brought him from over the North Sea, from Norway, to Ireland and released him here in this loveliest of woods, in Derrycairn Wood.

And here again an implied contrast, between Fionn mac Cumhaill who brought the blackbird and St Patrick who, coming later, brought the bronze hand-bell.

(*Night Journey,* pp. 243–6)

The Digging Fork
— *On Eros and the Wound* —

I once dreamed that Tristan was dreaming of Dionysus, and the Great Loosener said this to the young man:

> *Zeus incubated me in his thigh,*
> *My mother ripped apart by lightning.*
> *When he cut open his thigh he delivered*
> *A sexual wound to all men thereafter.*
> *Not all are gods who can sew it up*
> *With pins made of gold.*

I was pleased to see some skilful digging has already been done by Moriarty in related areas. I've gathered some of it here, and find it especially original. He comes at the terrain of Eros and the wound with autobiography and visioning. I admire especially the interior ruminations. It was very late in life, at the release of Birthday Letters, *that Ted Hughes wished he'd* stated a few feelings publicly years earlier. I think the move between personal and intensely mythological has something of the gear changes of Yeats about it, though I'm not sure if John would thank me for that.

A dream that John recounts begins with him entering a strip club on Old Compton Street. Admittedly, being a Moriarty dream we won't stay there for long. Soon there will be prehistoric creatures, and a great stretch of water that suddenly becomes an abyss and all manner of revelation. But for the reader, an initial revelation is the disclosure that John visited strip clubs at all, even in his youth. That he was led by desire to do so, led by his hips.

As John dreams, he is aware he is carrying a four-pronged fork, a digging fork. Sometimes he claims it has cow dung on it, sometimes dinosaur. Something about desire is utterly essential, utterly ancient, utterly primordial. Walking through Soho holding his shitty stick, his karmic fork, he walks into another realm altogether. The persistence of the dream for Moriarty, the circling round it again and again he did, means I included it here. And from there we move out into the area of both love and trouble. With his sensuous nature being as it was, he can write as lovingly about a mountain or antelope as he can a person, maybe more so. But it is wrong to see him as immune to attraction or love of humans, far from it.

From the largeness of his mother's charisma to women he loved along the way, John is not mocking or transcendent of human care. It may be that in the end he was wedded to something else, but earthy love got underneath his breastplate and laid its scarification on his heart. He's always clear about that.

Fairy tales tell us that if you can't speak your desire, then nothing much will happen. There needs to be articulation, no matter how clumsy. Inuit myth tells us that the whole world was formed from the desire of Wolverine for his beloved, One-Who-Wriggles-Nicely. Horniness has sacrality to it. Care and compassion also. John's shamanizing of philosophy and myth can initially take up most of our bandwidth, but suffused throughout is a man who understood longing, betrayal and to take oneself, 'to the end of passion'. In the end, John's perception of human love is that it's something that reaches out to touch the wider world, beyond the human. Otherwise *we place too much weight on the marriage. Actually, it makes us a little neurotic. A little nuts. A couple stand back to back, not just caught in the hypnosis of each other's gaze. Moriarty quietly discloses that his essential marriage is to what he calls 'Divine Ground', but he never shames what is human, romantic, earthly.*

>Rib in her, rung,
>
>The male route in her too
>Was the roost for Christ's love.
>
>Under Christ's high fist
>And falconer's glove
>
>The grave alone
>Can circumcise
>
>The bit that breaks down
>The mare's mouth in her thighs.

The Fisher King was wounded in the thigh. I was a wounding from the thigh. My phallus was a sensuousness that had grown around a savage horn, a wounding unicorn's horn. A sensuousness that had grown around the lance with which a rough Roman soldier opened a wound in Christ's side, making him androgyne.

A lance. And a unicorn's horn. And every month the wound I had opened in woman was a red weeping.

Horse was id in me, Jesus was inhibition in me. Horse in me fought Jesus in me, centaured me against Jesus in me. And my fear of what I might do to woman, my violence towards woman, opened its vulva lips at me, just looked at me, and I got the message.

Phallus in me was a falconer's wrist against sexual sensuousness in me.
A roost in me.
A night roost for Horus.
The falcon God of Egypt.

A night roost for Jesus, the Falcon God of Christendom.

Where did all this trouble come from? How did it all come about that an instinct so fundamental was so fundamentally plagued? How come that the need in me to be a man walking home from a dance with a woman was so infested with chonyid imaginings? Prarabdha Karma a Hindu would say. Seeds of things done and thought in previous incarnations ripening into awareness now. The voice which I, as Adam, heard in the garden was the voice of the Dr Bluebeard I had been. That could well be. In my search for answers I was often vulnerable to such an explanation. Was often willing to inherit and own such an explanation. But I don't know. One night I dreamed: I'm in the great square farmyard at home. On one side is the dwelling-house, on the other below by the animal houses, are big women. Tall women. Marvellously black. They are dancing. Sensuous as seaweed in a gently moving sea. They are dancing towards me. And I am walking towards them. When we are near each other one of these big women comes out of the troupe and comes towards me, dancing. We embrace. Phallically I can feel her skirt. The skirt between me and her becomes a board. I wake.

A board between phallus and vulva.

A board between me and my instincts.

A board between me and Africa.

A board between me and my sensuousness.

A board between me and this dream woman. A fine African woman. A Kikuyu woman. A woman from the Mountains of the Moon in Africa.

Woman.

Women.

Moving like seaweed in the moving sea of their own sensuousness. The dream was over. I was awake. I was thinking of the yard I grew up in. The sensuousness of Africa, my own last sensuousness had come to embrace me there tonight.

Embraced.

Embraced by Africa.

THE DIGGING FORK

Embraced by Africa on the very place where we ourselves used to kill the pig.

Killing the pig was frightfulness. Jack Scanlan, the gentlest man on the Bally Road, he was the pig killer. He'd come into the house with a big knife and a big hook. Himself and a couple of other men would go out to the piggery. Catching a pig by the ears Jack's assistants would pin it to the wall while Jack hooked it, underneath, between its jawbones. Ropes were tied to its legs front and back. And then pulling relentlessly on the hook and ropes the men gave it no choice but to walk their way. Not far from the front door of the dwelling house it was tumbled over onto its side. The underside of its neck near its collarbones was scalded with boiling water, the hair thereabouts was shaved by Jack with his big knife and then when the pig was immobilized by the men pulling on the hook and the ropes the neck was opened and the knife pushed in till it opened the heart. That night the pig would be hanging, opened and cleaned like Rembrandt's ox, from a big cross beam in our big farmhouse kitchen.

Sir Thomas Browne has written that: we carry with us the wonders we seek without us: there is all Africa and her prodigies in us.

Africa had come to me and embraced me there where twice every year a pig was killed. Why there? And why the board between me and the woman? Was it that I was protecting her from the pigkiller's knife in my phallus. Or was it that I was protecting my phallus from the savage mare's mouth in her thighs? The feeling I have is that I was doing both. The pigkiller's knife and the savage mare's mouth were mirror images of each other. Mirror images of the same terror-of-aggression-towards.

Lying awake in bed that night I supposed and supposed and supposed and supposed …

Supposing that as a child I too had fears of castration. I had seen my sisters and I feared that that which had been done to them might be done to me. I had seen my mother bleeding there and I couldn't explain it, or could I? I had seen what grown-ups had done to the pig. Maybe I'd be next on the yard.

My fear of their castrating knife became a knife of phallic aggression in me. And so the board. That board was me protecting the woman from me. That's what I thought that night lying awake in bed.

In spite of the shapes that haunt me, hawk-shapes, knife-shapes, lance-shapes, horn-shapes, mare-shapes, in spite all of them there is always in me a will to be one day a Shulamite shepherd to a Shulamite woman, a Red Indian Elk Man to a Red Indian Star Water Woman. A will in me that in spite of everything a song of songs will break out of me.

Moving like seaweed in the gently moving sea of their own sensuousness. But maybe I won't always meet that sensuousness, frightfully, in a frightful yard. Maybe the pigkiller's knife will fall from my phallus. Maybe one day I will be Adam and she will be Eve and we won't hear the voice of the Bluebeard I have been calling out in the garden.

For most of us, maybe, Adam and Eve belong to our future, not to our past.

We must all become the primal pair.

In a garden of Eden where, under the roots of the tree of life, asleep there, the serpent is Kundalini.

A serpent that tempts us to be men and women. That teaches us to be man and woman. That delights in us who're delighted now to be man and woman.

In this great Eden the animals name us. They name us man and they name us woman.

'My beloved spoke and said unto me, rise up my love, my fair one, and come away. For, lo, the winter is past, the rain is over and gone, the flowers appear on the Earth, the time of the singing of birds is come and the voice of the turtle is heard in our land.

'My beloved is mine and I am his, he feedeth amongst the lilies. Until the day break and the shadows flee away, turn, my beloved and be thou like a roe or a young hare upon the mountains of Bether.

'Behold thou art fair my beloved, yay, pleasant, also our bed is green. The beams of our house are cedar, and are rafters of fir.'

Eden and Arcady.

A *Vollard Suite* of centaur in me, Minotaur in me, Unicorn's horn and pigkiller's knife in me.

Eden and Arcady

Gethsemane and Vrindavan.

Gethsemane in Eden. Gethsemane in Arcady, Gethsemane in Vrindavan. And Picasso's *Vollard Suite No. 94* is the most heartbreaking vision I know of Adam walking towards Holy Thursday. And I know the young girl. When I was a lion's den she walked into me and told me I'd be alright.

A *Vollard Suite* of our growing.

And Engwura of shewings.

A Julian of Norwich night of therianthropic shewings.

Gethsemane night when we see and are Guernica.

Gethsemane night when we see and are Minotauromachie.

Gethsemane night when we see and are a centauromachie.

Gethsemane night when we see and hear Andromeda, Europa and Pasiphae singing:

> All shall be well
> And all shall be well
> And all manner of things shall be well.

Eleusinian Epoptae of all that we are. Ajanta Epoptae of all that we are.

There is all Africa and her prodigies in us. All cosmic and pre-cosmic deeps are in us.

And across the slow millennia since he emerged, man has been a hunter of animals with spears and with bows and arrows. He therefore has reason to know that wherever there is an open bleeding there must have been a wounding. Woman bleeds. Woman must have been wounded. And anxious about his aggression, a Stone Age hunter might have dreamed that he was the one who had wounded. And this little hunter, if there such was, is alive and well in me. His fear and his guilt and his strange dream logic are alive and well in me. Maybe everyone's infancy is the infancy of the race all over again. For whatever reason, I've suffered sometimes from an awful sense of some awful ancient havoc at the sight of the genitals. And that's why the pit in Lascaux is as if it were a pit in my psyche. To go down into it, imaginatively, as I often do, is to go down into a pit of unconscious cerebration become pictorially manifest in the famous scene of the sexually speared bison bull and the felled, ithyphallic birdman. Attempting to explain this scene, Leroi-Gourhan reminds us that there is a psychological assimilation of phallus to spear, of vulva to wound. How generally true this is I do not know. Nor do I know how relevant, if at all it is to the Palaeolithic picture. It is, however, relevant in a revelatory way I feel to a dream I dreamed a few years ago.

There are three of us, a man, a woman, and myself. I am between them and we are walking back along the shore of the upper lake in Glendalough. We have been to St Kevin's cell and we have prayed there. Suddenly I'm aware that something acutely embarrassing is happening to me, a sword is falling out of my phallus. In pain and shame I bend down seeking to retrieve it before it clangs, accusingly, on the hard, black tarmacadam path. But no, I don't succeed, and it clangs, it clangs, it clangs. Although they have already observed what has happened, the man and the woman aren't at all surprised, or upset. I wake up. The next day I contact the woman and I tell her the dream. In prayer that evening, she sinks into a trance-like state. She is on the path by the upper lake. She comes upon the sword. Picking it up she, she holds it, lying horizontally, in both of her hands, and she prays, asking the heavens that, they being gracious, it will never again afflict any man in the way that it afflicted me. As she stands there, holding it, praying, a ray of light reaches down from on high and, touching it, dissolves it.

Thinking of this dream and its sequel I have questions to ask: is there, if only in the form of unconscious cerebration, a maimed Fisher King in every man? However Palaeolithically pit-deep it might be, is there Fisher King trouble in every man? And what kind of trouble is it?

Did our forebears in medieval Europe misdiagnose it and did they as a consequence fail to heal themselves of it?

What ails the Fisher King? Did he indeed suffer from a psychological assimilation of phallus to spear, of vulva to wound? Is that the unconscious content that possesses him, inducing in him a dread of his wounding potency? Or, alternatively, inducing in him in him a dread of his wounding horn? If Picasso's Femme Torero etchings were carried before him in the nightly procession; if indeed the drawings of the bull erotically goring the horse were carried before him, would he know, looking at them, that the question the questing knight must ask was already answered? If so, I imagine yet another attempt, an attempt in our day, to heal him: leading him down into an unsuspected cave-pit in his castle, our Galahad holds up a Guernica lamp, illuminating a Palaeolithically painted wall. That's your trouble, Galahad says, pointing to the spear in the bull's sexuality, in male sexuality.

He draws it out.

The bull is healed.

The king is healed.

Revived, the birdman stands up and, taking his staff, he sings healing here in the hurt totemic depths of our psyches.

The rhinoceroses come back.

Healed and underground, healed overground.

In the Waste Land everywhere there are stirrings of life.

(*Turtle, Vol. 1*, pp. 18–23)

A dream: I am walking in Soho. I turn into Old Compton Street. A few doors down I walk into a striptease club. I've been here many times. I know the place well. As I expected, the striptease is going on upstairs. I can hear the music. The ground-floor has changed. And I am surprised. I look on in wonder. Instead of the lurid billboards and equally lurid lady at the reception desk I've been used to, there are now five or six long rows of clothes racks. And all the clothes are unisexual. It is this that causes me to be in a state of silent wonder. I see no one. I'm aware of my own aloneness. I leave.

Walking up Wardour Street, I've a four-pronged farmer farm fork in my hand. There are scales of dry cow dung on the prongs. I'm no longer in the city. I'm in an eighteenth-century park. It becomes a vast savannah. There's a patch of ground that looks different from its surroundings. I begin to dig. I uncover three granite steps. I climb down. Reaching the lowest step I find myself looking down on an oceanarium. On the other side, so far away I can hardly see him, I see a man standing at the edge of the water. Bending down he touches something under the surface of the water. Whatever it is he touches begins to rise. Effortlessly, of its own accord, it rises. In a moment I see what it is. It's a great iron grid. It rises out of the water. Something vast, something suppressed, is rising beneath it. Continuing to rise, the grid folds itself flush with the embankment I'm standing on. Up from the floor of the ocean below, I see immensity rising. As it rises, I see it's an immense tangle of living things. Draped across it, undulating, so that now it is manifest and now it isn't, is a great snake-form. It's a dogfish I say. That's what it is. It's a dogfish. Never have I seen anything so stupendous. Underneath its outrageously arrogant skin are tropics and tundras and taigas and summers and sunsets and dawns of aliveness. All the dreams the galaxies haven't yet got around to dreaming are there. The undreamed in the dreamed, the manifest in the unmanifest, the noumenal and the phenomenal, the night of Brahma, and the day of Brahma undulations of the same Great Ouroboros. The suppressed Ouroboros rises and under its undulations, rising, is an immense tangle of living things.

Far away and far, far below at the edge of the oceanarium I am. I'm standing where the man originally stood. I think that I am that man. An otter comes towards me walking. It would be a calamity, I feel, were he to bite my small toe. I withdraw my foot out of harm's way. The otter passes me. He doesn't bite.

I'm sitting on the water. An abyss it is now, not an ocean. Without looking I see that there's a great Mesozoic reptile behind me. It is mindless

THE DIGGING FORK

and ugly. It is getting ready to lunge at me and swallow me. It makes vicious, darting movements in every direction. Then it steadies itself, facing me. It opens its vast, mindless mouth. This is it I think. I'm finished. But there's nothing I can do. I could only wait. It opens its mouth still wider. It lunges furiously towards me, but at the last moment, when I'm already in the shadow of the deepest pit of perdition, it veers away becoming as it does so a harmless, shy, little animal going about its business. I wake up.

At the time I dreamed this dream I most desperately needed good news about me. And now at last my psyche was saying fear not. The repressed had returned and I hadn't gone mad. That much I more or less instantly understood.

Later I was tempted to think that the dream had implications for our religious past.

I imagined a religious past in which

> Marduk didn't slay Tiamat,
> Apollo didn't slay Python,
> Yahweh didn't slay Leviathan.

'Twas if all the dragon-slaying gods of the ancient Near-and-Middle East had heard Jesus. At the end of his night in Gethsemane, Jesus commanded Peter to put up his sword. At this moment Peter wasn't only Peter the apostle. He was every dragon slayer who had at any time attempted to lobotomize the psyche, to lobotomize the Earth.

Is it possible that after Gethsemane we should think not of Yahweh slaying Leviathan but of Yahweh lying on the coils of Leviathan.

Is it possible as Hindus think of

> Vishnuanantasayin

so we can think of

> Yahwehleviathasayin.

Anyway, Beast and Abyss aren't as incorrigibly hostile as we've imagined them to be.

We don't need to slay the one or to set up bars and doors against the other.

The repressing grid can go up, the restraining bars and doors can give way, and we aren't destroyed.

The repressing grid went up in Job, the restraining bars indoors gave way in him, yet there he is, the one through whom we inherited the promise:

'For thou shalt be in league with the stones of the field, and the beasts of the field shall be at peace with thee.'

We have a new past to emerge from.

(*Turtle*, Vol. 1, pp. 30–2)

In the course of their many adventures, Tristan and Isolde came to share the same bed one night, but to make sure that they would be chaste, they placed a sword between them.

When, as a young man it was my turn to be Tristan in a similar situation, it was out of my phallus not from my scabbard, that I drew the sword. Not inhibiting then, or for two decades later, it was there nonetheless. She didn't see it. I didn't see it. How indeed could either of us see it, it being so deeply buried in my Palaeolithic, Fisher King's unconscious.

I was in trouble. I knew it, yet I wasn't at all aware of it, even though I wrote about it. As in a dream, the images and symbols it emerged in, revealed it yet concealed it. How different in this regard am I, I sometimes wonder, from other men. The medieval knight, parfait and gentle, has a sword hanging from his hip. In the great Wild West of a modern collective dream the Lone Ranger shoots from the hip. A rock band calls itself The Sex Pistols. And at the frontier also of his own primitive instincts, the young Punk wears a savagely studded leather belt slung suggestively and aggressively low over his crotch. There is, apparently, evidence to suggest that 'colg' the ancient Irish word for sword does sometimes also mean penis, and 'truaill' the word for sheath or scabbard has a secondary, metaphorical reference to the vagina. And the primary meaning of the word 'vagina' is sheath. Ithyphallic in hundreds of silos, America and the Soviet Union threatened each other with orgasms of destruction.

A sword in their bed between a man and a woman. Where in Christ's name did it come from? We know of course for what conscious reason it is there. But is there another reason? An unconscious reason? A reason as old as the crypt in Lascaux? A sense I have, looking at the famous scene of the bison bull, the birdman and the rhinoceros, for I take it that the rhinoceros is of the scene, is that it depicts a disaster of awful continuing consequences at or near the foundation of psyche in the human male.

In Arthurian literature we read of a dolorous stroke that destroyed the Realm of Logrys. As I read it, without of course being able to adduce supporting evidence, the stroke depicted here destroyed commonage consciousness, not everywhere, but here in Europe. This means that animals cannot now be our Totemic Ancestors. In that rhinoceros all the animals of our Pleistocene Serengeti are walking away. It also means that shamanism is dead. Gone with the animals are their medicines. The bird staff will decay leaving us to cope alone as best we can, with our diseases.

As for the spear that is thrust through the anus, bowels and penis of the bison bull, Leroi-Gourhan asserts, seeking an interpretation, that there is a psychological assimilation of penis to spear and vulva to wound. Whether or not this assimilation has relevance to the scene we are discussing I do not know. I do know, though, that it has almost shocking revelatory relevance to sexual trouble in me. It names the trouble. And I sometimes think that it also names the sexual trouble of the Fisher King. So much that I think of the crypt in Lascaux as the crypt in the Grail castle.

The Fisher King suffers. For this reason I suggest: it was inevitably into our own sexuality also that we thrust that spear and it has lodged there as an impulse. The impulse is older than the spear thrust but since the spear thrust, and as a consequence of it, it is in us more acutely now. Not in everyone. In whomsoever, in any generation, is Fisher King.

Oedipus has given his name or his name has been given, to sexual trouble in some human males. But your quest hasn't come to an end in that discovery, Sigmund: there is trouble altogether more terrible and more ancient. There is Fisher King trouble. On your way to his crypt you will come one night, as Gawain came, to Chateau Merveil. In it you will retire to sleep in a bed called Le Liz de la Mervoille. All night long you will be attacked, by a rhinoceros attacked, by a bison bull attacked, by spears attacked, the spears being a proliferation of the Palaeolithic spear we once thrust through the anus, bowels or penis of an animal ancestor.

Le coup douloureux. La lance qui saigne.
Le riche Roi Méhaigné.

Can you heal these Pleistocene depths of our psyches, Sigmund?

OR

The animals of our lost Serengeti gone, their medicines gone with them, their totemic sheltering is gone with them, do we need the Divine more than the physician?

Tristan and Isolde.
Venus and Adonis.

Adonis and the birdman.

In every generation the bull and boar will charge. From within our own depths they will charge, the bull with mane erect, the boar with frothy mouth.

With his horn the bull will gore the birdman, with his tusk the bull will tread Adonis.

Ours is the horn, ours is the tusk, ours is the wound.
Doing to the boar what we did to the Minotaur will not work:

> There now he liveth in eternall blis,
> Joying his goddesse, and of her enjoyed:
> Ne feareth he henceforth that foe of his,
> With which with his cruell tuske him deadly cloyd.
> For that wilde Bore, that which him once annoyd,
> She firmly hath imprisonéd for ay,
> That her swete love his malice mote avoyd,
> In a strong rocky Cave, which is they say,
> Hewen underneath that Mount, that none him loosen may.

We might think of that cave as Lascaux. In our day we suffer from troubles altogether older than the troubles that erupted during the night of royal nuptials in Thebes.

You must go farther back, Sigmund. Farther down and farther back. As far down, as far back as the boar hounds went, as Venus went. You must see what she saw:

> … the wide wound that the boar [has] trenched
> In his soft flank …

For:

> 'Tis true, 'tis true; thus was Adonis slain:
> He ran up upon the boar with his spear sharp,
> Who did not whet his teeth at him again
> But by a kiss thought to persuade him there;
> And nuzzling in his flank, the loving swine
> Sheathed unaware the tusk in his soft groin.
> Making him androgyne.

Making him experience what since the beginning Venus herself has experienced: the vagina is the sheath the bull puts his tusk in, the bull puts his horn in.

A HUT AT THE EDGE OF THE VILLAGE

Before Oedipus was the Maymed Kynge is.
In his castle the lance bleeds, the horn bleeds, the tusk bleeds.

    Lunarly, his wound bleeds.

All of which will seem like fantasy floating free from fact, although Jung perhaps did not think so:

> We must never forget our historical premises. Only a little more than a thousand years ago we stumbled from the cruellest beginnings of polytheism into the midst of a highly developed oriental religion which lifted the imaginative minds of half-savages to a height that did not correspond to their degree of spiritual development. In order to maintain this height in some fashion or other, the instinctual sphere inevitably had to be repressed to a great extent. Thus religious practice and morality took on a remarkably violent, almost malicious character. The repressed elements naturally do not develop, but vegetate further in there anginal barbarism in the unconscious. We would like to scale the heights of a philosophical religion but are, in fact, incapable of it. To grow up to it is the most we can hope for. The Amfortas wound and the Faustian split in the Germanic man are not yet healed; his unconscious is still loaded with those contents which must first become conscious before he can be liberated from them.
>
>   (*Turtle, Vol. 1*, pp. 74–7)

Silver-Branch Beholding
— *On Hugeness* —

Any real encounter with Moriarty's work is going to involve entering the hugeness. That's the only word I can find for it. When Merlin wandered out from the forest of Caledon it was rumoured he could speak seventy languages. There's something of that going on here. It derails us for the most part: some doors swing happily open, while others remain resolutely locked. There does not appear to be one drop of ink spent smoothing out the terrain between his leaps. What a blessing. We should remember where we are – the hut at the edge of the village. John is crooning his chant over our beguiled heads to be 'sore amazed' at the workings of creation again.

He's walked a thousand miles in the rain to bring these things to us.

There is a Lakota phrase, 'too much great spirit', that cautions on spending too long fasting in holy places. That there can be no shore left to return to, no village fire, no dark beer, no warm bed, just immensity. You may taste that sometimes. You may wish to read them as a Persian reads Hafez, in an almost divinatory manner, rather than ploughing through with a ruler and set square. Such devices tend to disintegrate on impact.

But there is the kind of reward that comes when you have been called to a mysterious forest, summoned your nerve and started to visit a holy place within it. One day you turn around and there's a little path with your footfall, there is a track made strong by your fidelity. Revel in the hugeness. Myth makes things bigger, not smaller, madder not tamer, in the hope that writ-large we really start to wrestle with the angels again. This is how the Earth talks to us.

We say of ourselves that we live in a world. But it would perhaps be truer to say that we live in a tale told.

> A tale told by Aztecs,
> A tale told by Maoris,
> A talc told by Hapiru
> A tale told by persons who call themselves scientists.

The tale told that Vikings lived in had, as all such tales have, a beginning, a middle and an end.

The end as they imagined it was stupendous. They called it Ragnarok. To announce it three cocks crow:

> A cock called Fjalar crows in the birdwood,
> A cock called Goldcomb crows within hearing of Valhalla,
> A cock called Rustred crows at the bars of Hel.

And it begins:

> And now it is Axe-time and sword-time,
> Wind-time and wolf-time

It is time when, weary of restraining him in its depths, the Earth yawns, releasing Loki and his hordes into their hunger and thirst and lust for universal destruction.

It is time when, bursting the chains that bind him, and running free, Fenriswolf opens his mouth and with it, foaming already, he takes the measure of Earth and sky. And he howls, and he howls, and he howls, and the third time he howls he has it, the third time he howls he knows he has it, he has their measure.

Everywhere now there is war. To exist now, to be now, is to be a war. There is war in all, and between all, the nine worlds that are in Yggdrasil, the World Tree. There is war between cosmos and chaos.

In the end there is nothing, neither cosmos nor chaos. There is only Ginnungagap, the Great Yawn, the Great Emptiness.

> It is a mysterious Emptiness, though,
> It is an Emptiness that somehow seeds itself,
> In time it will be a pregnant Emptiness,
> In time a new Universe will be born from it.

A tale told. A tale that sheltered Vikings on the high wild seas between the Faroe Islands and Iceland, sheltered them and housed them on the no man's nowhere of icebergs and fogs between Iceland and Newfoundland. And who knows! Echoes of it might yet haunt the Viking foundations of Dublin.

We don't, therefore, need to import such words as Ragnarok and Ginnungagap into Ireland. They, and their cognates, were spoken and heard beside the Black Pool long before the Germanic dialects of the Angles and Saxons had evolved into English. They are old Dublin words. And the sibyl, the spakona, whom the Vikings set up and enthroned in Clonmacnoise, she too might have spoken them, speaking them there at the monastic heart of the country. They are Irish words. It is time, maybe, that we reclaimed them.

I do not know whether or not the universe undergoes a Ragnarok. And if it does I do not know whether it undergoes it the way that Nordic spakonas and volvas say that it does.

Certain it is, though, that there are persons who undergo an inner Ragnarok, a psychic Ragnarok. In the course of undergoing it, shaken now at their foundations, they come to see that, conscious and unconscious, psyche in them is an eclipse. An eclipse asleep. An eclipse awake. An eclipse of thinking, imagining, hearing, seeing, touch, taste and smell.

It's a seeing, it's a realization, that shatters us, deeply, in our deepest, self-conscious foundations.

It is now a time of great woe.

It is I-am-sore-amazed time.

It is I-am-sore-broken-in-the-place-of-dragons time.

It is I-am-a-brother-to-dragons-and-a-companion-to-owls time.

It is wide-breaking-in-of-waters time.

It is dark-night-of-the-soul time.

It is passive-dark-night-of-the-spirit time.

It is time to listen to St John of the Cross. He can speak to us, he can comfort us, he has been through it, he has left logbooks, the best there are.

No rock of faith presenting itself, it is time for the abyss of faith.

It is time for total surrender to Divine Good shepherding.

I cannot find you, God. And the reason I cannot find you is simple: it is with that in me that eclipses you that I seek you.

> I can't sense you or know you or name you, God.
> I can't find you inside me or in the world outside,
> But I still want to be your servant. God.

Our faith is abyssal now. Our praying is abyssal: may I be as out of your way awake God as I am in dreamless sleep.

Our final homecoming isn't our doing. It is God's doing.

Ragnarok and Ginnungagap are words that have meaning on our way home.

They are words we might speak again in Clonmacnoise. Born as they are out of our initial Job and Jonah terror they aren't, in the end, appropriate words. The good words are

Dark Night of the Soul
and
Divine Ungrund.

So ask not for whom Fjalar crows. Ask not for whom Goldcomb crows. Ask not for whom Rustred crows.

They crow for you.

They crow to remind you of the glorious homecoming that awaits you.
(*Dreamtime*, pp. 103–5)

The big myths and the big wisdom stories are a root language that survived the mutations and dispersals of Babel.

It is a language that challenges us to live etymologically towards depths and heights and towards Divine Ground beyond them, and how sad it is that we so rarely speak it or, as Heidegger might say, how sad it is that we so rarely allow ouselves to be spoken by it.

More frightening than sad is that it is fast becoming a foreign language or, worse maybe, a dead language.

The truth is, the demise of a major modern language would be of little import compared to its demise.

Its demise means Madame Sosostris dealing in cards too inane to be wicked, too dull to be voyant, let alone clairvoyant.

Measuring his life, not in rites of passage, but in coffee spoons, Prufrock is portent.
(*Night Journey*, p. 524)

Instead of doing the lazy thing, instead of assimilating Jesus to an available and convenient archetype, what a better apocalypse it would be were we to endure the full shock of Him as a neotype.

In Him, after so many invalidating false starts, we have found evolutionary legitimacy.
(*Night Journey*, p. 163)

In Auschwitz, Blake's *Songs of Experience* sound like *Songs of Innocence*.

In Auschwitz, we look at the relative harmlessness of Tyger and we ask, did He who made him make us?

In Auschwitz we ask, did He who made the merely killing poison of the cobra make our poison?

In the pit in Lascaux we ask, did He who gave Tyrannosaurus the power to reproduce himself give us the power, the spear-raping power, to reproduce our- selves? And if so, why? Why a being so incompatible with the rest of creation? Did God turn against His own creation in us? Are we the agents of His hatred of His own creation?

Answering God who talked to him out of the whirlwind, Job might have said, You are wasting your divine time challenging me to look at Behemoth and Leviathan. Behemoth I have had for my breakfast and Leviathan is the candle I light my way to bed with. Challenge me rather to look at real terror, challenge me to look at myself.

And, God bless us, there are among us innocents who think we are something that a socio-political revolution can remedy, sorting us out in all that we are, finally and forever. So excited by his final solution was Isaiah that it didn't occur to him to consult his own reptile brain:

> And the sucking child shall play on the hole of the asp, and the weaned child shall put his hand in the cockatrice's den.

Could it be that neither cockatrice nor asp will be all that impressed by our more or less brainless optimism on their behalf?

It is what our phylogenetically fulsome myths know: any part of our psyche that we aren't bringing with us isn't behind us, it is ahead of us, waiting to trip us up.

Think of Pasiphae, how she was tripped up. Think of Oedipus, how he was tripped up.

And Actaeon: a hunter of animals, he was one day engulfed by the unintegrated animal in himself.

And always, if we are to have an adequate sense of ourselves, we will need to know ourselves more deeply than myths do.

All things considered, Jesus crossing the Torrent is our best bet. Dropping our bullfighter's cape as He crosses into Gethsemane and dropping the chatelaine's luf-lace as He crosses onto Golgotha, He is our best evolutionary bet.

*

How perilous it is to be versatile in mythic self-awareness. How perilous it is not to be versatile in mythic self-awareness.

*

How flabbergasted we are, how flabber-aghasted we are, when we find that the Minotaur myth is our address. How flabber-aghasted we are when we find that the Actaeon myth is the house where we live at the end of our lane. What now can we do but seek asylum in the final enormities of Christ's Passion and death and reabsorption into God.

Think of it, Pasiphae seeking asylum in Gethsemane.
Think of it, Actaeon seeking asylum in Gethsemane.
Think of it, Oedipus seeking asylum in Gethsemane.
Think of it, all three of them seeking asylum on the self-naughting Nunatak.

The enormities of our liberation suggest the enormities of our captivity. The captivity not just of our humanity, the captivity it mostly is.

*

As Songs of Experience our myths are woefully wanting, and yet how superficial our lives must be if we do not need them in the more or less ceaseless business of negotiating a working deal with ourselves.

*

Could it be that, of those who cross into Gethsemane, some will find themselves undergoing an anagnorisis into mythic self-recognition?

Could it be that someone who believed that his good manners reached to the core of him will now find himself saying, Pasiphae I am, Actaeon I am, Oedipus I am, the Fisher King who can only generate a Waste Land I am?

*

The Fisher King in his Waste Land is finale to Gilgamesh in the Cedar Forest and in this we see that there is an anagnorisis that Gilgamesh did not undergo.

*

Think of it, the anagnorisis that Sophocles or Shakespeare, had they thought about him, would have scripted for Gilgamesh.

*

Think of the phallus that was carried in procession at festivals in honour of Bacchus in ancient Greece. It was called the ithuphallos, meaning the straight phallus. It is because of the dagger in it that Macbeth's phallus is as ithyphallic as Tarquin's.

It happens in war: as they bayonet each other men find that they are sexually aroused, sometimes to the point of erection.

Did it happen to the Fisher King, and this truly dreadful unanimity of sex and murder, however occasional or rare it might be, was it by this that he was afflicted?

Be that as it may, what is sure is that the Fisher King's coat of arms is in full display in the Palaeolithic pit. It shows the genitally speared bull overthrowing us in what was our first ecumenically successful attempt to be human.

Not of course that it is a coat of arms exclusive to the Fisher King.

Given how he became king and how he conducted himself as king it would be entirely appropriate for Macbeth to fly it from his battlements.

But then why stop here? Why not extend the franchise to Everyman?

Is it not appropriate that he, Everyman, should fly it from his chimney too?

Indeed, until he does so how can we claim that our quest to heal the Fisher King has been accomplished?

It is Merlin who comes to Camelot and announces the spearless regeneration of the world:

> 'Know, Arthur, that in thy time the most sublime prophecy that was ever made has been fulfilled; for the Fisher King is healed, the spell under which Britain has languished is broken, and Perceval is become Lord of the Grail. From now on he will renounce chivalry, and will surrender himself entirely to the grace of his Creator.' When the king and his knights heard this they began to weep with one voice, and to pray God that he would bring it to a favourable conclusion.

The spell broken.

The spell which, for all our revolutions, reformations, renaissances and enlightenments, kept us fast-bound in spear-cast culture proliferating across the world in varieties of John Locke Lands, Willy Loman Lands, Waste Lands all.

So demiurged by spear-cast culture was Job that it was only in being broken that he broke out of it. In the end, tectonic shock after tectonic shock having done the work, it was through a breach big as himself in himself that he walked out into the first world, a world of obdurately grand and obdurately wretched savageries.

Sad to say, Job only learned the obduracy. Seeing past it, seeing through it, he didn't go on to become an ostrich dreamer, a Behemoth dreamer, a Leviathan dreamer.

As a Tiamat dreamer, as a Yam dreamer, as a Leviathan dreamer, as an Apophis dreamer, as a Python dreamer, Job would be a new past from which a new pre- sent and future would grow.

We could even imagine Job as a thunder dreamer.

Sitting in his blue thunder tipi at the heart of our biblical way of being in the world, he drums his thunder drum and he sings his thunder songs.

Europe, A Prophesy. America, A Prophesy.
We have emerged from spear-cast culture.

(Night Journey, pp. 201–4)

The Grail and the Silver Branch, each of them in its way inviting us to set out in quest of paradisal perception, each of them in its way letting us know what Blake would have us know, that when the doors of perception are cleansed we will see everything as it is, infinite. Not just abstractly infinite of course. Infinite in the way that the Silver-Branch singing of an atom is infinite.

Altogether more astonishing than seeing things as they are is hearing things as they are, and in that sense audition of the Silver Branch leaves us yet more profoundly dumbfounded than vision of the Grail, even though it is with a crakynge and a cryynge of thundir that it comes among us.

*

More important than all his fabrications to Homo faber are the Karmic Digging Fork, the Tenebrae Harrow and the Silver Branch. It is with them, not with the wheel or the test-tube, that we will evolve.

*

The Grail and the Silver Branch.

Our quest for a more open vision of the Grail, our quest for Silver-Branch seeing and knowing.

Hardly had the Grail, covered as it was in whyght samyte, passed out of the Hall of the Round Table in Camelot on Pentecost Sunday than Sir Gawain came to his feet:

> 'Now', seyde sir Gawayne, 'we have bene servyd thys day of what metys and drynkes we thought on. But one thyng begyled us, that we myght nat se the Holy Grayle: hit was so preciously covered.

SILVER-BRANCH BEHOLDING

> Wherefore I woll make me here a vow that to-morne, withoute longer abydynge, I shall laboure in the queste of the Sankgreall, and that I shall holde me oute a twelve-month and a day or more if need be, and never shall I returne unto the courte agayne tylle I have sene hit more opynly than hit hath bene shewed here. And iff I may nat spede I shall returne agayne as he that may nat be ayenst the wylle of God.'

Inspired by his example other knights came to their feet and so it was that on the morrow

> ... they toke their horsys and rode thorow the streete of Camelot. And there was wepyng of ryche and poore, and the kynge turned away and might nat speke for wepyng.

What a beau geste! What a fair deed!

But a yet fairer geste, a yet fairer deed, it would be to set out in quest not of exceptional vision of the extra-ordinary but of lasting vision of the ordinary. Having emerged into Silver-Branch seeing and knowing, we only have to catch sight of a fence-post covered in lichens and now, our quest accomplished, we turn our horse round and come home.

*

Our planet in the state that it is, it follows that for every one of us who sets out on the Grail Quest, there should be hundreds setting out in quest of the Silver Branch.

*

Manannán mac Lir, a Celtic god. Morgan le Faye, a Celtic goddess.

Our rendezvous with Manannán mac Lir at sea. And, on land, our rendezvous, at one remove, with Morgan le Faye.

What else but this can Celtic Christianity be? What else can it be but a Christianity that is hospitable to Manannán mac Lir's song at sea and to Morgan le Faye's lila on land. A Christianity that is hospitable to the Silver Branch and to the Tenebrae Harrow. A Christianity that is hospitable to Silver-Branch seeing and knowing and to metanoesis.

*

The Silver Branch, the Karmic Digging Fork, the Tenebrae Harrow: if only by way of aspiration, shouldn't they figure in our efforts to distinguish and define ourselves as a species?

*

The Branch, the Fork, the Harrow: in heraldic display, they would signify us in our availability to evolution.

*

Emblazoned on the banner under which he rides north, the Branch, the Fork and the Harrow would signify that Sir Gawain had come to a new understanding of what, in anticipation of it, he called his 'anious vyage'.

*

Could it be that Sir Gawain declined an invitation to meet Morgan le Faye because, pious Christian that he was, he feared a relapse to pagan polytheism?

How could someone meet Morgan le Faye and not end up conceding and believing in her divinity?

How could someone meet Cú Roí mac Dáire walking south through Ireland with his gigantic Churl's head under his gigantic Churl's arm and not concede and believe in his divinity?

How could someone see Manannán mac Lir at sea, see him and hear him singing to us out over the manes and heads of his chariot horses, and not concede and believe in his divinity?

How could we blame someone who came back not just polytheistically credent but polytheistically evangelical from such encounters?

Did Sir Gawain not know that in riding north he was riding back into the domain of the old gods?

Out of need perhaps, Yeats declared that until the Battle of the Boyne Ireland belonged to Asia. Could it be that in translating the Upanishads he was therefore in his own mind engaged in a work of restoration? It is likely that *Sir Gawain and the Green Knight* is not an attempt at such restoration and yet there is everywhere in the story a sense of pagan eruption and it wouldn't be outlandish to suggest that Sir Gawain gets and endures a pagan answer to his Christian prayer.

> The knyght wel that tyde
> To Mary made his mone,
> That ho hym red to ryde
> And wysse hym to sum wone ...

> 'Cros Kryst me spede,' he prayed.

Even at the risk of a relapse into polytheism, how can we not learn from Manannán mac Lir at sea and from Morgan le Faye on land?

A Christianity that learns from Manannán and Morgan le Faye must be very different from a Christianity that learns from Plato and Aristotle.

Think of Plato's experience of things as imitations, as shadows, and then think of Manannán's experience of them, in all ways and in all conditions, as ontologically resonant and radiant as the Silver Branch.

Think of Yeats, think of his Silver-Branch experience of himself:

> My fiftieth year had come and gone, I sat, a solitary man,
> In a crowded London shop,
> An open book and empty cup
> On the marble table-top.

> While on the shop and street I gazed
> My body of a sudden blazed;
> And twenty minutes more or less

It seemed, so great my happiness,
That I was blessèd and could bless.

And there was a day when, out of the blue behind the grey, or should we say, there was a day when, out of the blue that grey is both resonant and radiant with, Jacob Boheme saw a pewter dish as Manannán would see it.

*

That's it, Wallace: thirteen ways of looking at a blackbird suddenly exalted into one way of seeing a pewter dish in a shoemaker's shop in Gorlitz or into one way of seeing an empty cup on a marble table-top in a teashop in London.

*

Unlike poets of the blue guitar, poets of the Silver Branch only have to report what they see. And they don't need to ride out as Sir Gawain did. The pewter dish right there in front of them in their shoemaker's shop, that's it, that's the Holy Grail, and it isn't covered in whyght samyte, or if it is look for it not on the Grail but in the doors of perception.

*

What is so strange is that before we sought it the Grail sought us. Also, before we sought it the Silver Branch sought us. We are being sought. But, given the noisesphere of our own creation that we live in, we are making it almost infinitely difficult to be found.

Where there is no vision the people perish.

Exceptional is Bran Mac Feabhail who, a Silver-Branch ontology the consequence, yielded to what for him was an inexplicable need for silence and solitude.

*

SILVER-BRANCH BEHOLDING

Sad it is that, Silver Branch and Holy Grail having come to us, here we still are riding in his chariot with Marduk not in his chariot with Manannán.

*

Leuwenhoek with his microscope, Galileo with his telescope, neither man having seen the pewter dish, the Holy Grail, they drank their soup from.

*

Manannán, the Muse of poets.
    Manannán, the Muse of science.
    Manannán, the Muse of
              Scientia Mirabilis.

*

Darwin's voyage to a theory of evolution is a matter of little consequence compared to Bran's voyage to Silver-Branch ontology.

*

Having sailed with Fitz Roy in the Beagle, it remains for Darwin to sail in his curchán with Bran.

*

The Silver Branch is a finer truth about the universe than $E=mc^2$.

*

Having written *The General Theory of Relativity*, it remains for Einstein to write a Zohar, a Book of Splendour, a book of three assertions:

    Every bush is a burning bush.
    Every stone is an a-stone-ishment turned in on its own rose window wonders.
    As is every star so is every cancer cell a sefirah.

*

Manannán mac Lir and Morgan le Faye. Manannán inviting us and, maybe from behind the scenes, guiding us, to Silver-Branch ontology. Morgan le Faye inviting us and, maybe from behind the scenes guiding us, to metanoesis.

*

Bran's voyage to Silver-Branch ontology and Sir Gawain's vyage to metanoesis: even if we set up house in another solar system, in another galaxy, or in all galaxies, this voyage and this vyage will continue to be our evolutionary future.

In Francis Bacon's terms, advancement local is not an evolutionary substitute for advancement essential.

*

Vishnu teaching Narada
    Manannán teaching Bran.

Morgan le Fay teaching Sir Gawain

And, in so many of us, Miranda turning into Medousa.

For the moment let us enjoy the privilege of not being philosophically consistent. With Manannán we learn to apprehend things as things. With Morgan le Faye we learn to apprehend things as phainomena, as fata Morgana. With Vishnu we learn to apprehend things as maya. With Medousa we have declined into Ulro.

For the one who is able for it, plurality of apperceptive apprehension is liberation not dispersal.

But, given how easy it is to get carried away, we must not ascribe undue value to such liberation. Even when it has become a permanent condition, paradisal perception isn't entire re-entry into Paradise. The emergence of Miranda in us doesn't forever preclude the emergence of the Minotaur in us.

*

Sooner or later in the course of advancing essentially we will come to a dip in our road that is as deep and as wide as the Grand Canyon. Nietzsche came to it:

> I have discovered for myself that the old human and animal life, indeed the entire prehistory and past of all sentient being, works on, loves on, hates on, thinks on in me.

With this discovery we are back among the phylogenetically regressive possibilities enacted for us in Greek myth, or if we are Christians baptismally assimilated to Him, we are back sore amazed with Christ in Gethsemane.

But Nietzsche didn't only come to a dip deep as Gethsemane in his Antichrist's road. Having crossed into it, he recoiled from the frightful but nonetheless blessed calamity of Good Friday at noon:

> I suddenly woke up in the midst of this dream, but only to the consciousness that I am dreaming and that I must go on dreaming lest I perish – as a somnambulist must go on dreaming lest he fall.

Jesus asked three of His disciples to watch with Him, to stay awake with Him but, being as little able for final liberation as Nietzsche was, they too took refuge in sleep.

I can see it, Jesus coming to Nietzsche in the dip in his Antichrist's road and saying to him what He said to His disciples:

Sleep on now.

(*Night Journey*, pp. 367–73)

REVELATION

Famously, Michelangelo claimed that instead of imposing an image of Bacchus or of Christ upon stone he rather found them already in it, and all he had to do was to release them.

A Christ we hear about in a gnostic gospel would agree:

> Split the rock he says, and I am there
> Split the log and there also you will find me.

In this we have moved from image to reality. The Divine, in other words, is everywhere in nature, in goat and Capricorn, in pike and Pisces, in lion and Leo, in crab and Cancer. And those masterful Cambodian sculptors, did they too feel that they were merely releasing its Buddha's smile of enlightenment from stone?

Looking at Torc Mountain as I walk towards it today, I sense that this smile is the innermost and outermost truth about things. Even about the mouth, wide open and roaring to Tyrannosaurus rex.

Michelangelo released Bacchus, a god who is latent in it, from stone.

Cambodian sculptors released the enlightenment that is native to it from stone.

Time to release the Earth Goddess,

Buddh Gaia,

from stone.

Only not of course *from* stone. The thing finished, stone chipped away, will continue enthused by the Divine within itself.

And so, to anticipate: there She is, the Revealed Wonder, first sight of Her assuring us that we are

BUDDH GAIANS.

(*Night Journey*, p. 615)

A question early Christians asked with passionate urgency was: who in his nature, who in his being, in his substance, was Jesus? A very Aristotelian question to which, at Chalcedon, there was given a very Aristotelian answer.

There is, however, another, not less passionately urgent question these same seeking Christians might have asked: who, as experiencer, is Jesus? Who as experiencer who has crossed the Kedron, is Jesus? Is he, having crossed the Kedron, utterly unique, utterly without analogy to anyone or anything, so that we cannot, as a consequence, talk about him? Or, given the fullness of humanity in him, can we not assume that there are archetypes to which, if only partially, we can assimilate him, seeking to know. We mustn't assume, a priori, that the most hospitable archetypes will be biblical.

Maybe there is no room in the archetypal Middle-Eastern inn. No room, maybe, in the archetypal Mediterranean inn, in the archetypal European inn, in the archetypal Christian inn.

A lonely man.

A man sore amazed.

A man whose intuitions and experiences caused him to be archetypally unaccommodated, archetypally unassimilable?

A man religiously and culturally out at heel, out at elbow, out at medulla, out asleep, out awake.

A man with whom, philosophically or mythologically, his culture couldn't watch.

As the fourth Evangelist, had he so perceived it, might have put it: made flesh, The Word was verbally unhoused.

There are persons whose vision of things isn't culturally validated, isn't, in their lifetimes, culturally assimilable. Of itself, their vision of things excommunicates them.

If the gospels say sooth, however, experiencing himself archetypally disenfranchised wasn't a sorrow the Man of Sorrows was acquainted with.

On the contrary, it is, Christians believe, his willingness, in obedience, to be the archetype he was and knew himself to be that most characterizes him. It is his willingness to stupendously enact, to stupendously endure, the stupendous consequences of being the Incarnate Archetype he was that so religiously appals, so religiously delights, them.

And Jesus returned in the power of the spirit into Galilee: and there went out a fame of him through all the region round about. And he taught in their synagogues, being glorified of all. And he came to Nazareth where he had been brought up: and, as his custom was, he went into the synagogue on the Sabbath day, and stood up for to read. And there was delivered unto him the book of the prophet Esaias. And when he had opened the book, he found the place where it was written. The Spirit of the Lord is upon me, because he hath anointed me to preach the gospel to the poor; he hath sent me to heal the broken hearted, to preach deliverance to the captives, and recovering of sight to the blind, to set at liberty them that are bruised. To preach the acceptable year of the Lord. And he closed the book, and he gave it again to the minister, and sat down. And the eyes of all them that were in the synagogue were fastened on him. And he began to say unto them. This day is this scripture fulfilled in your ears. And all bare him witness, and wondered at the gracious words that proceeded out of his mouth. And they said, Is not this Joseph's son?

He was Joseph's son. Sure, he was. But placating a neighbour whose gate was lying there uncompleted didn't preoccupy him now:

> Then certain of the scribes and the Pharisees answered, saying. Master, we would see a sign from thee. But he answered and said unto them, an evil and adulterous generation seeketh after a sign; and there shall no sign be given to it but the sign of the prophet Jonas: For as Jonas was three days and three nights in the whale's belly; so shall the Son of man be three days and three nights in the heart of the Earth. The men of Nineveh shall rise up in judgment with this generation, and

shall condemn it: because they repented at the preaching of Jonas; and, behold, a greater than Jonas is here.

Greater than Jonah.

Greater not just as a prophet, we presume. Greater, also, in that, when his time comes, he will be more able than Jonah was for the Jonah initiation.

Out at sea, in a tempest, Jonah was thrown overboard. Swallowing him, a whale turned flukes and sounded, carrying him down under the roots of the mountains, under the roots of psyche and universe, not under them as two realities, under them as one reality, because, at root, at centre, and at summit, psyche and universe are one and the same.

Jonah was carried down into the Great Deep under experienceable reality. He was carried down into the Great Deep that was before the psyverse was. The Great Deep. Hebrews call it Tehom. Hindus call it Turiya. Turiya is Nirguna Brahman, the Brahman without attributes, the Divine Ground that is groundless, and out of which, in playful delight, the psyverse emanated, back into which, sensing bliss, it will return.

For all its emanative vastness, the psyverse hasn't left, hasn't emerged from, the Divine Ground it is emanating from. When it wakes from the dream of its emanations, it will know that it never left home.

And when he returns, the raven that Noah sent out will bring good news.

To Christians, Muslims, Jews, to all peoples who don't yet know, the raven, returning, will announce

Tehom is Turiya.

Carried down under the roots of the mountains, carried down, subjectively that is, under the roots of awareness-of, the weeds of the Great Deep, of Nirvikalpasamadhi that is, were wrapped about Jonah's head.

And Jesus, Joseph's son, says of himself that he is greater than Jonah. Clearly, an immense spiritual breakthrough is at hand.

Greater than Jonah.

Greater than Job. More able than Job for the Job initiation.

Job and Jonah are rites of passage. In Jesus, these initiations, these rites, were sanctified. In Jesus, in him, and through him for us, these rites, these initiations, became religiously available, religiously safe.

Job was a good man. Civically and domestically, he was rock solid. So habituated in an unquestioning, unconscious way was he to conventional living that there was little or no trace of irrational, first or pristine nature in him. From his core out, calmly and contentedly, Job was honourable, acceptable civic second nature. At evening, Job would sit in the big city gate, being wise, conventionally. He was much given to proverbs.

Suddenly, as if in the night while he slept there had been a wide break- ing-in of waters, civic, domestic living was swept away, and Job awoke, his proverbs no use to him now, at the frontier.

Job had come before himself.

The self he had come before was a King of Terrors.

Nights now when Job was a brother to dragons and a companion to owls.

Nights now when hell was naked before him; when, before him, within him, Destruction had no covering.

Nights now, when, like it or not, Job must drink the wine of astonishment. Nights now when, drinking it to its dregs. Job must drink the cup of trembling.

A man inwardly clairvoyant to all he inwardly was, behemothically.

A man sore amazed.

A man sore expectant of what had already come to pass: a man sore expectant of abyss and beast irruptively from within.

A man sore broken in the place of dragons.

His religion couldn't watch with him. Wise only in the wisdom of its city gates, civilization couldn't watch with him.

Job was in trouble. Job was at the frontier.

The untameable God of all untameable frontiers, inner and outer, a theologically untameable God, a God before whom Hebrew prophecy and Greek philosophy were without arraignable resource, a God who, whatever else he was, was Pashupari, Lord of animals – this terrifying Lord of all untameable frontiers, this Lord of animals, this Lord of Abyss and Beast, confronted Job, commanding him to take stock of himself, as a man, before daystars, abyss and beast.

Job's biblical bluff was called. With unlobotomized mind, with unlobotomized eyes. Job beheld the unlobotomized Earth.

When they passed before him in Eden, Adam named the animals.

When, more brutally but also more bounteously, they passed before Job, Job, falling silent, shook dust and ashes on his biblically betrayed, biblically blessed head.

For recovering of sight to the blind, Jesus came.

For us, as for Job, this means the falling away like scales from our eyes, the falling away like *idola tribus* from our eyes, of verses twenty-six and twenty-eight of Genesis, chapter one.

Jesus, Joseph's son, came to set at liberty them that are bruised epistemologically by their naive realism.

It was claimed for Jesus, Joseph's son, that, genetically, he was of the royal line of David.

Crossing the Kedron, his genetic ancestry doesn't count for particularly much.

His ancestors now are Job and Jonah.

It is to Job and Jonah, in the fullness of their de-vast-ating experiences, that he will be experientially assimilated.

And because he is greater than Job, greater than Jonah, the Job and Jonah rites of passage will enact themselves more comprehensively and more inwardly in him than we have been biblically prepared for in the biblical versions of the Job and Jonah initiations.

The names 'Job' and 'Jonah' aren't only names of two fictional characters in the Bible. Like the name 'Osiris' in ancient Egyptian religion, they are generic names. They are the names of all those people who, while they are undergoing them, undergo the Job and the Jonah anagnorises.

Nowadays, in many societies, it is expected of persons that they will become inimitable, unique individuals. There have been and are societies, however, where a contrary outcome to our growing was or is desirable. Archetypalization not individuation is the goal. In medieval Christendom, for instance, there were persons who, in the hope of becoming an Alter Christus, another Christ, attempted, sometimes with fierce ascetic determination, to suppress or eliminate what was unique and individual in them. And in ancient Egypt, a person, having died, was sacramentally assimilated into the image and likeness and post-mortem destiny of Osiris. So complete was the assimilation, that the person was sometimes referred to as the Osiris.

Having crossed the Kedron, Jesus, while remaining uniquely himself, is also, in experiential assimilation, a Job who is greater than Job, a Jonah who is greater than Jonah.

Rites of passage enacted themselves in Job and Jonah.

In plenary realization of their inherent possibilities, these rites of passage re-enacted themselves in Jesus, and in him in whom there was sorrow but no resistance, they opened out into a continuous way through into the bliss of self-loss in Divine Ground.

We are heirs, if we choose, to this way through.

And, as a consequence,

> We are, most humbly, heirs with Hindus to Upanishads.
> We are, most humbly, heirs with Buddhists to Sutras.
> We are, most humbly, heirs with Taoists to the
> Tao Te Ching.
> We are, most humbly, heirs with Christians to
> Evangel and Evangelanta.
> We are, most humbly, heirs with Jews to heard of and unheard of
> Books of Splendour.
> We are, most humbly, heirs with Sufis to Bezels of Wisdom.
> We are, most humbly, heirs with Navajo to sacred circles and songs.
> We are, most humbly, heirs with Siberian, Inuit and Aboriginal
> shamans to sacred songs.

SILVER-BRANCH BEHOLDING

Jesus crossed the Kedron.

There is a way through for us, when we are ready. When they are ready, for stars.

(*Dreamtime*, pp. 39–43)

Crossing the Torrent
— *On Christianity* —

John Moriarty attempts to move Christianity into new ground for almost all of us. Even with his love of other traditions, his deepest unfolding is into the luminosity of Christ, the coal-black darkness of Christ. He repeatedly returns to a key thought: that we remain awake with Christ, rather than fall into the disciples' slumber in Gethsemane, and promotes the assistance of two rituals – Ephphatha and Tenebrae – to assist with our fidelity of presence. Ephphatha translates as 'be opened', which John encourages not with anguished vigilance but with wu-wei, a kind of effortless flow. I think he's sensitive to our neurotic tendencies.

Embedded like magical sigils throughout are his personal energy centres – seal holes – and a progression towards the Christian experience he calls Bright Angel Trail. The ceremony of Tenebrae takes us into a nourishing darkness, not a well-lit, big-tent revival, and Moriarty's way does not spare us Auschwitz, the Gulags, or Ahab mad on the boat, screaming for Moby-Dick.

John's familiarity with his own relationship to this emergent Christianity can lose us if we're not careful. We are sometimes chasing a leaping hare, not a bridge-builder. Unless there is some previous engagement with the esoteric dimensions of Christianity, it's a big ask to not start flicking the pages.

But we would do well to not worry about that. We would do well to simply retrace our steps through this long grass. A perpetual return leading to a perpetual freshness.

I enjoy reading him out loud, in small chunks, preferably with a few like-minded souls. There's a contemplative dimension in Moriarty's work that invites us not to tear at it madly but give it spacious attention. If we attempt to swallow the ocean we drown, but a salty drop dabbed on our forehead may be a great blessing. John's Jesus is an embodiment of what he calls 'a new kind of human success', but a success drawn from Jesus shuddering his god-psyche through the deepest of sufferings. Deep myth takes human form and cracks the world open.

There is a pummelling urgency in all of this, Moriarty calling forth the comparison of Merlin forming the Round Table, such is the need for 'a small immensity of the new Christian epoch'. And how do we begin our graduation to this new Christian epoch? By demonstrating our willingness to welcome it, to invite the hugeness of God into our fragile lives.

The visioning Moriarty had for this was suitably ambitious: a healing of our relationship to the wider Earth and its occupants, even renaming the world as Buddh Gaia, the alternative being a swift disintegration of our sensuous and devotional relationship to all life. That there is no nutrition in the current utilitarian model, that we need to humbly consume the canyon-deep, bitter herbs of our past mistakes and behold again this heavenly life, the Silver-Branch perception he spoke of so many times. To John this was a Jesus path.

Moriarty disables the contemporary makeover of Christ as this affable teacher amongst many others, singles him out, digs with his karmic stick into Jesus's life and work until he hits real, disturbing psychic ground. Psychic life. Disturbing in the sense that Christ's words start to shake the tree again. Mountains sing, rocks get rolled away. Jesus no longer looks European and mild, but dark, powerful and under an awful lot of pressure. This is Jesus in the long black coat, this is Jesus of the strange words and the hard demands, this is Jesus a-wild. This is not fat, blond, rich American Jesus, this is terrifying Jesus. If we even dare glance in his direction, the Good News may feel like the very Bad News for some considerable time. Walt Whitman said we contain multitudes, but maybe we contain legions too.

In his letter to Ephesians St Paul says that as well as ascending above all the heavens Jesus descended into the lowest parts of the Earth.

Let us imagine this descent.

In Arizona, in the American south-west, is the Grand Canyon.

Geologically immense in its rock walls and scree slopes and mesas and side-canyons, it is within itself a vast world two hundred and eighty miles long, four to eighteen miles wide from rim to rim and, descending through the accumulated sediments of thirteen ancient seafloors, it is a vertical mile deep. Under these seafloors, eating a yet deeper way for itself through rocks two thousand million years old, is the sometimes savagely cascading Colorado river, dropping ten thousand feet from source to sea. In a descending series from rim to river the old exposed seabeds, geological strata now, are called Kaibab, Toroweap, Coconino, Hermit, Supai, Redwall, Muav, Bright Angel, Tapeats, Shinumo, Hakatai, Bass and Vishnu. Starting well below the Mesozoic screeches of a pterosaur in featherless, bald-bodied flight, Bright Angel Trail takes us down through all thirteen seabeds, the deepest of them metamorphosed into dark schist, illuminated by intrusions of pink magma.

Not immediately companionable are magma and mind.

Not immediately companionable are Redwall and religion.

And yet, enforcing companionableness, we have named the mesas within the Canyon for goddesses and gods, themselves not at first sight companionable. At random, they are called the Vishnu Temple, the Brahma Temple, the Deva Temple, the Shiva Temple, Diana Temple, Vesta Temple and, cut down to human size, the Buddha Temple, the Zoroaster Temple, the Castor Temple, the Pollux Temple.

In the Canyon above all, ichthyosaurs swimming in seas two hundred million years above us and ammonites managing to move across seafloors two hundred million years beneath us, it surely isn't entirely wise to assume that nature will respond in kind to our naive naming. Will Shiva, by residing in it, divinise the mesa we have reserved for him? Will Vishnu lighten the burden of matter to maya? Or, the next time we walk under a rock wall will we still imagine what would happen to us if it fell on us? Can maya hurt maya? And even if it can, there is on this understanding of things no reason to be upset, for the hurt itself is an illusion.

Quite obviously, religion colonized the eggs of a pterosaur at no cost to itself. Quite obviously, religion colonized the perfectly orthodonted mind of Tyrannosaurus rex at no cost to itself.

Quite obviously, religion colonized the Canyon in all its rock walls and falls at no cost to itself.

But, in the event that we believe that evolution is synonymous with moral improvement, there right before us is something that will give us pause, a living rattlesnake coiled about a fossilized trilobite, and that not just anywhere, that on Bright Angel shale.

The rattlesnake and Bright Angel.

What will Bright Angel think and do?

Will he think of the rattlesnake as everything that frustrates human wishes and will he do accordingly? Will he do what Marduk did? Marduk slew and sliced Tiamat, did it in a way that converted chaos to cosmos. Will he do what Atum the Egyptian Sun god did? Nightly in the underworld Atum decapitated Apophis, the terrible, bellowing snake-dragon sitting superlatively tall on his thousand coils. Will he do what Baal did? Thinking of Yam, the Abyss-Beast, as insatiably hostile to cosmos and culture, he rode out, he too, in his storm chariot and, as he so boastfully claimed, did successful final battle with him. Will he do what Yahweh did? Breaking the superbly insurgent seven heads of the Abyss-Beast, now called Rahab or Leviathan, Yahweh fed him to the flesh-famished peoples of the wilderness.

Given that divine precedent isn't wanting, what will Bright Angel do? Will he in his insecure hatred of him magnify rattlesnake to Tiamat size, to Apophis size, to Yam size, to Leviathan size? Will he turn dragon slayer? Will he, in effect, lobotomize Earth and psyche, settling for lesser, less threatened, less frightened life? For tri-lobe-ite life? Or, ultimately, for lobeless life? For life unconscious of self and other-than-self. Or, at the very most, for life as we lived it in Babylon, Luxor, Jerusalem, Athens, Rome?

What are we to do?

Do we reproduce the Canyon as a Colosseum and say, here on summer afternoons, is fullness of civic-savage life?

Since, from the slaying of Tiamat till now, our world has been a Colosseum without walls, and since in consequence we are facing into ecological collapse, it would be sapient of us, would it not, to give ourselves a second chance with the Canyon?

Which, for reasons bearing yet more deeply on our condition, is what Jesus undertook and achieved.

As St John the evangelist says, he crossed the Torrent.

As St Paul says, he went down into the lowest parts of the Earth.

So it wasn't just the Kedron he crossed. Going all the way down to it, he crossed the Colorado, into our further and final evolution. In the opening chapter of his gospel, St Mark has this to say about Jesus:

> And it came to pass in those days, that Jesus came from Nazareth of Galilee, and was baptized of John in Jordan. And straightway coming up out of the water, he saw the heavens opened, and the Spirit like a dove descending upon him: and there came a voice from heaven, saying, Thou art my beloved Son, in whom I am well pleased. And immediately the Spirit driveth him into the wilderness. And he was there in the wilderness forty days, tempted of Satan; and was with the wild beasts; and the angels ministered unto him.

Almost always it happens: no sooner the heavens opening above us than the hell worlds opening beneath us, no sooner angels ministering to us than Satan testing us.

And not only was Jesus with the wild beasts. Inwardly, out there in the wilderness, he was with all that is beastly in us.

CROSSING THE TORRENT

Not many nights would have passed when, like Job, he might have said, I am a brother to dragons and a companion to owls.

Remembering the Psalm, he might have said, Thou hast sore broken me in the place of dragons and covered me in the shadow of death.

Two nights later, again remembering, he might have said, Thou hast made me to see hard things, Thou hast made me to drink the wine of astonishment.

Later that night, out there in the Judaean badlands, he might have said, Thou hast made me to drink the dregs of the cup of trembling and wring them out.

A phrase of six words,

and was with the wild beasts

Properly read, short though it is, that phrase is two hundred and eighty miles long, it varies from four to eighteen miles wide, from rim to river it is a vertical mile deep.

And there is yet more.
What Jacob Boehme came to know, that Jesus endured:

In man is all what so ever the Sun shines upon or heaven contains, also hell and all the deeps.

What Sir Thomas Browne came to know, that he endured:

In our humanity we are a compendium of the six days, a cosmic compendium.

What Joseph Conrad came to know, that he endured:

The mind of man is capable of anything – because everything is in it, all the past as well as all the future.

Suffered before God and towards God, such plenary self-endurance is passion and, to begin with Jesus had no choice in it, either to go towards it or to recoil from it:

the Spirit driveth him into the wilderness

Coming back from the wilderness in the power of the Spirit he overturned our world, with parables.

That done, this time by choice, a pterosaur flying fifty million years above him, he set out, down along Bright Angel Trail, down towards the Torrent thirteen and three-quarter karmic miles below.

Divining what he had in mind, the gods and goddesses came to their temple doors and, knowing that what he was doing had never been imagined let alone undertaken, they did as much as they dared to do, they wished him well.

So passionately red were all rock walls, it seemed that the Earth itself was willing him to do what he was doing.

Go down, Jesus

Go down, Jesus

Go down, Jesus

Go down into the lowest parts of the Earth, down below humanity, down below mammal, down below reptile, down below amphibian, down below fish, down below ammonite, down below alga, down below the first protein.

By the Torrent down there, in a depth where I is we, Bright Angel is waiting. He points to a rockpool that mirrors the thirteen and three quarters miles of stratified karma. Going down on his knees, Jesus cups his fin-fraught hands down into the water. When the water in this improvised chalice has settled and is again mirroring the karma of the ages he brings it to his lips and drinks it, to the lees, leaving nothing to wring out. All the while he has been doing this the Earth has been coming up over its own karmic horizon and there it is now

    Gaiakhty

Next day, on the self-naughting Nunatak still within the Canyon, at a height where I is we, where the individual is cosmic compendium, he looked down into the universal empty skull and there it is now

    Buddh Gaia

    brightening the universe

Our creed is simple:

    Jesus is the world's new story
    All the way forward from its beginnings it is a

NEW WORLD

And the challenge to us is

INNOVATION

fully acknowledging that Jesus geologically endured the evolutionary mutation of the Labyrinth into Bright Angel Trail, fully acknowledging that Jesus has claimed the whole Canyon for culture, the whole psyche for sanctity.

    (*Slí Na Fírinne*, pp. 17–21)

Much as we might ask of a boat, is it seaworthy? so might we ask of the human psyche, is it worldworthy. More seriously, we must ask, is it selfworthy? Is it able for itself? Is it able for its own enormities? As Sir Thomas Browne might ask, is it able within itself to be a compendium of the six days? Is it able, relying only on what it is in itself, to be consciously a compendium of the six days? And, on the assumption that it is in fact a compendium of the six days, across how much of it and down into how much of it does the ego's jurisdictive writ run?

We can guess, given what he knew, what Jacob Boehme's answer would be:

> In man is all whatsoever the Sun shines upon
> or heaven contains, also hell and all the deeps.

We can guess, given what he knew, what Gerard Manley Hopkins' answer would be:

> O the mind, mind has mountains, cliffs of fall
> Frightful, sheer, no-man-fathomed. Hold them cheap
> May who ne'er hung there ...

We can guess, given what he knew, what Joseph Conrad's answer would be:

> The mind of man is capable of anything – because everything is in it, all the past as well as all the future.

We can guess what, in their phylogenetic engulfment, Pasiphae, Andromeda, Hippolytus, Actaeon and Oedipus would say.

Permanent and complete engulfment such as Coatlicue underwent is one of the risks we run when we cross the Torrent with Jesus.

Should we therefore not so much as think of crossing it with him?

The truth is, given how we are constituted, we are at risk irrespective of where we are, idling here or seeking there, as little aware as we can be on this side of the Torrent or fully aware on the far side of it.

What to do?

Do we do what Peter, James and John did? Do we take refuge in sleep?

Then cometh Jesus with them unto a place called Gethsemane, and saith unto the disciples, sit ye here, while I go and pray yonder. And he took with him Peter and the two sons of Zebedee, and began to be sorrowful and very heavy. Then saith he unto them, my soul is exceeding sorrowful, even unto death: tarry ye here, and watch with me. And he went a little further, and fell on his face, and prayed, saying, O my Father, if it be possible, let this cup pass from me: nevertheless not as I will but as thou wilt. And he cometh unto the disciples, and findeth them asleep, and saith unto Peter, what, could ye not watch with me one hour? Watch and pray, that ye enter not into temptation: the spirit indeed is willing, but the flesh is weak. He went away again the second time, and prayed, saying, O my Father, if this cup may not pass away from me, except I drink it, thy will be done. And he came and found them asleep again: for their eyes were heavy. And he left them and went away again, and prayed the third time, saying the same words. Then cometh he to his disciples, and saith unto them, sleep on now, and take your rest: behold, the hour is at hand …

Imperilled by a double discovery, Nietzsche took refuge in sleep:

I have discovered for myself that the old human and animal life, indeed the entire pre-history and past of all sentient being, works on, loves on, hates on, thinks on, in me.

I suddenly woke up in the midst of this dream, but only to the consciousness that I am dreaming and that I must go on dreaming lest I perish – as a somnambulist must go on dreaming lest he fall.

Jesus chose precisely otherwise. Crossing into Gethsemane, he chose to awaken to all that we phylogenetically and extraphylogenetically are. Climbing to the place or summit of the skull, he chose to wake up from waking.

In the light of this, how solitarily awe-ful are his words:

> sleep on now

As for us, there are good reasons to choose as Nietzsche chose and there are good reasons to choose as Narada chose.

Vishnu's gentle stay on his eagerness notwithstanding, Narada would awaken.

And to some of us, if not yet to all of us, Christ's invitation remains:

> tarry ye here, and watch with me

And St Paul sees our baptism not just as an invitation to watch, he sees it as an invitation to undergo:

> Know ye not, that so many of us as were baptized into Jesus Christ were baptized into his death? Therefore we are buried with him by baptism into death: that like as Christ was raised up from the dead by the glory of the Father, even so we also should walk in newness of life.

To Romans he says,
> now it is high time to awake out of sleep

Extending its meaning mystically, this we can understand to be saying,

> now it is high time to do what Jesus did
> now it is high time to look down into the empty skull
> now it is high time to walk back through the rent in dualizing consciousness
> as it deludes us asleep and awake.

The question remains: how seaworthy is the human psyche? We only have to remember how suddenly it opened at the seams in Job and Jonah:

When I say my bed shall comfort me, my couch shall ease my complaint, then thou scarest me with dreams and terrifiest me through visions, so that my soul chooseth strangling and death rather than my life.

The waters compassed me about, even to the soul: the depth closed me round about, the weeds were wrapped about my head. I went down to the bottoms of the mountains: the Earth with her bars was about me for ever ...

Push not off, is Ishmael's advice.

And yet how can we live with the three most terrible words ever addressed to us

      sleep on now

Nietzsche and Narada.

Nietzsche's choice as perilous perhaps as Narada's.

What to do?

That the Earth is an evolutionary success all the way forward from its beginnings is an opportunity for us to be other than how we have been. Indeed, if the Earth is to continue brightening our corner of the universe we must be other than how we have been.

Starting from the lowest parts of the Earth, Jesus pioneered a trail all the way back to the Divine Source. He pioneered it for all things, for stegosaurus and rhinoceros as well as for mollusc and Moses.

In the interest of our further and final evolution we need to select this trail. As nature selects a favourable mutation we need to select it. Suggesting enormities, we need to select it as nature has selected metamorphosis in insects. Not that the trail is a matter merely of transformation, of transition from one to another form. It is something fearfully and marvellously more.

The best way or maybe the only way to select the trail is to reconfigure it into ritual, into legomena and dromena, into sacred things sacredly said, into sacred things sacredly done.

Fortunately, we already have a ritual which, with some adjustments, meets our need. We have

Tenebrae

The name is variously derived from the canonical accounts of Christ's Passion, St Luke's for instance, in Latin:

*Erat autem fere hora sexta, et tenebrae factae
sunt in universam terram usque in horam nonam.
Et obscuratus est sol: et velum templi scissum est medium ...*

And it was about the sixth hour, and there was a darkness
over all the Earth until the ninth hour. And the Sun was darkened,
and the veil of the temple was rent in the middle ...

As it was traditionally performed, Tenebrae was the ritual in which we watched with Jesus from the moment he crossed the Torrent until, on the third day following, he reappeared in the Garden of the Sepulchre.

Briefly, this is how it was enacted.

A candelabrum, called the Tenebrae Harrow or the Tenebrae hearse, was carried in and set upon a standard in the sanctuary. Triangular in shape, it had seven candles on each ascending side and, making fifteen in all, a candle at the apex.

Sitting cowled in their choir stalls, the fully lighted harrow between them, the monks gave solemn and unhurried Gregorian voice to Christ entering upon his Passion. This they did chanting antiphons drawn from the great tragic psalms. A cantor chanted an entire Passion narrative. Building to a sense of final destructive desolation and abandonment, the Lamentations of Jeremiah were chanted. Concurrently with all of this, at prescribed intervals, a candle would be quenched. Finally, only the candle at the apex was still lighting and this was now taken down and taken round behind the altar and entombed there, leaving the church in darkness. So it was that we shook off sleep and watched with Jesus passionately pioneering a trail for all things. So it was that we passionately accompanied him all the way. So it was that we pioneered with him into the darkness of Good Friday. So it was that we abided in

Tenebrae

until, blazing upon us, the light of Easter would have utterly comprehended us inward and downward to the core and root of our brightening lives.

A great ritual. The greatest that humanity is heir to.

A ritual demiurgic to a new humanity.

A ritual that promotes us into and through our further and final evolution

Imagine it.

In baptismal assimilation to Jesus, he doing it for us, we cup our hands down into the mirroring rockpool on the floor of the Karmic Canyon. Next day, still within the Canyon, he doing it for us, we look down into the empty skull.

In this we very obviously aren't humanists relying entirely on our own resources. On the contrary. Always aware of how unseaworthy within itself the human psyche is, we at all times lay and hold ourselves radically open to Divine assistance. Indeed, given how inwardly precipitous we are, as in Pasiphae, Actaeon, Oedipus, we must be careful, especially on the far side of the Torrent, to not ask too much of ourselves and, above all, to not be over bold. Some there are who to their cost will have learned that every ladder continues gapingly downwards as a labyrinth and for that reason alone we have need of nothing less than the greatest of rituals, we have need of

Tenebrae

Imagine it, a seven-branched, or better
a nine-branched harrow

It is our senses and faculties that we quench on the way into

        the cloud of unknowing

on the way into

        the dark night of the soul

on the way into

        Tenebrae

Imagine it.

The Grail Quest accomplished, we set out on a new quest, the Tenebrae Quest, a quest to script and score a ritual which, being a way through, will see us through to blessedness in

        God

to blessedness in

        Buddh Gaia

        (*Slí Na Fírinne*, pp. 23–8)

Here, in Slí na Fírinne, our confidence in ourselves as Christians enables us, no matter what its provenance, to listen to the wisdom of humanity. While we do not relapse into polytheistic credence in doing so, we listen to a Bhagavad Gita sung to us at sea by the god of the sea. In it he challenges us to come out of the prison-house of common perception into Silver-Branch perception or, as a Christian would name it, paradisal perception.

In challenging us to emerge into Silver-Branch perception he is challenging us to emerge into Silver-Branch morality, into Silver-Branch behaviour towards all things.

        (*Slí Na Fírinne*, p. 33)

In the Gospel according to St Mark we see Jesus the healer at work:

> And again, departing from the coasts of Tyre and Sidon, he came unto the sea of Galilee, through the midst of the coasts of Decapolis. And they bring unto him one that was deaf, and had an impediment in his speech, and they beseech him to put his hand upon him. And he took him aside from the multitude, and put his fingers into his ears, and he spit, and he touched his tongue; and looking up to heaven, he signed, and saith unto him, Ephphatha, that is, Be opened. And straightway his ears were opened, and the string of his tongue was loosed, and he spake plain.

The Aramaic word stands out.

It is a word of three syllables, the stress falling on the first of them:

> Eph'-pha-tha

The question to ask here is: how deaf to the wonder and terror and glory of the world are those of us who can hear? How unable to express the wonder and terror and glory of the world are those of us who can speak?

Think of how Thomas Traherne experienced the world as a child:

> The corn was orient and immortal wheat, which never should be reaped, nor was ever sown. I thought it had stood from everlasting to everlasting. The dust and stones of the street were as precious as gold: the gates were at first the end of the world. The green trees when I saw them first through one of the gates transported and ravished me, their sweetness and unusual beauty made my heart to leap, and almost mad with ecstasy, they were such strange and wonderful things. The men! Oh what venerable and reverend creatures did the aged seem! Immortal cherubins! And young men glittering and sparkling angels. And maids strange seraphic pieces of life and beauty! Boys and girls tumbling in the street, and playing, were moving jewels. I knew not that they were born or should die,

but all things abided eternally as they were in their proper places. Eternity was manifest in the light of the day, and something infinite behind everything appeared, which talked with my expectation and moved my desire. The city seemed to stand in Eden, or to be built in heaven ... Famously, Wordsworth describes our declension from this, our first paradisal or celestial estate, into what he calls the light of common day:

> Our birth is but a sleep and a forgetting:
> The Soul that rises with us, our life's Star,
> Hath had elsewhere its setting,
> And cometh from afar:
> Not in entire forgetfulness,
> And not in utter nakedness,
> But trailing clouds of glory do we come
> From God, who is our home:
> Heaven lies about us in our infancy!
> Shades of the prison-house begin to close
> Upon the growing Boy,
> But He
> Beholds the light, and whence it flows,
> He sees it in his joy;
> The Youth, who farther from the East
> Must travel, still is Nature's Priest,
> And by the vision splendid
> Is on his way attended;
> At length the Man perceives it die away,
> And fade into the light of common day.

For all that, Edwin Muir reminds us that we can grow back, however briefly, into paradisal perception:

> Those lumbering horses in the steady plough,
> On the bare field – I wonder why, just now,

They seemed terrible, so wild and strange,
Like magic power on the stony grange.

Perhaps some childish hour has come again,
When I watched fearful, through the blackening rain,
Their hooves like pistons in an ancient mill
Move up and down, yet seem as standing still.

Their conquering hooves which trod the stubble down
Were ritual that turned the field to brown,
And their great hulks were seraphim of gold,
Or mute ecstatic monsters on the mould.

And oh the rapture, when, one furrow done,
They marched broad-breasted to the sinking Sun!
The light flowed off their bossy sides in flakes;
The furrows rolled behind like struggling snakes.

But when at dusk with steaming nostrils home they came,
They seemed gigantic in the gloom,
And warm and glowing with mysterious fire,
That lit their smouldering bodies in the mire.

Their eyes as brilliant and as wide as night
Gleamed with a cruel apocalyptic light.
Their manes the leaping ire of the wind
Lifted with rage invisible and blind.

Ah, now it fades! It fades! And I must pine
Again for that dread country crystalline,
Where the blank field and the still-standing tree
Were bright and fearful presences to me.

William Blake, it seems, didn't need to reacquire paradisal perception. No, it would seem, the shades of the prison-house didn't close upon him:

> The atoms of Democritus
> And Newton's particles of light
> Are sands upon the Red Sea shore
> Where Israel's tents do shine so bright

He assured us that if the doors of perception were cleansed, everything would appear to us as it is, infinite.

As for Yeats, it wasn't so much that he experienced a cleansing or an opening of the doors of perception, rather was it that he blazed ontologically:

> My fiftieth year had come and gone,
> I sat, a solitary man,
> In a crowded London shop,
> An open book and empty cup
> On the marble table-top.
>
> While on the shop and street I gazed
> My body of a sudden blazed;
> And twenty minutes more or less
> It seemed, so great my happiness,
> That I was blessed and could bless.

And there is that strange night not just of Silver-Branch perception but of ontological epiphany described for us in *Moby-Dick*:

> Days, weeks passed, and under easy sail, the ivory Pequod had slowly swept across four several cruising-grounds; that off the Azores; off the Cape de Verdes; on the Plate (so called), being off the mouth of the Rio de la Plata; and the Carrol Ground, an unstaked, watery locality, southerly from St. Helena.

It was while gliding through these latter waters that one serene and moonlight night, when all the waves rolled by like scrolls of silver, and, by their soft, suffusing seethings, made what seemed a silvery silence, not a solitude; on such a silent night a silvery jet was seen far in advance of the white bubbles at the bow. Lit up by the Moon, it looked celestial; seemed some plumed and glittering god uprising from the sea.

Tonight, on board a whale ship named for an exterminated tribe, we do not have to take Manannán mac Lir's word for it. Tonight we see and know reality as the sea god sees it and knows it. His Gita is the sea's Gita is our Gita. As he sings atoms sing, their auroral sonance their reality.

In a sense, it is what Manannán said to Bran:

Ephphatha
Be opened

Be opened in instinct, eye and mind and you will see that the physics of the Silver Branch is the physics of atoms, is the physics of rocks, is the physics of flowers, is the physics of stars.

His own transfiguration is Christ's Gita, is Christ's Zohar, an ontology. Press him on the issue on that day and he will tell you that not only is the lily of the field clad in glory, it is glory. Ontologically, it is glory.

Isaiah speaks:

In the year that king Uzziah died, I saw also the Lord sitting upon a throne, high and lifted up, and his train filled the temple. Above it stood the seraphims; each one had six wings; with twain he covered his face, and with twain he covered his feet, and with twain he did fly. And one cried unto another, and said, Holy, holy, holy, is the Lord of hosts: the whole Earth is full of his glory. And the posts of the door moved at the voice of him that cried, and the house was filled with smoke. Then said I, Woe is me! for I am undone; because

> I am a man of unclean lips, and I dwell in the midst of a people of unclean lips: for mine eyes have seen the king, the Lord of hosts. Then flew one of the seraphims unto me, having a live coal in his hand, which he had taken with the tongs from off the altar: and he laid it upon my mouth, and said, Lo, this hath touched thy lips: and thine iniquity is taken away, and thy sin purged. Also I heard the voice of the Lord, saying, Whom shall I send, and who will go for us? Then said I, Here am I, send me.

And what we wonder was his iniquity, what his sin?

What our iniquity, what our sin?

In the event that we are iniquitous, it must sure have its source in our inability or in our unwillingness to see that the earth doesn't only reflect God's glory, it is full of it, it is fun-filled, filled-full of it.

Where there is no vision, expect moral failure.

Contrarywise, where there is Silver-Branch perception and a sense of Silver Branch being, it is likely that there will be Silver-Branch morality.

It sometimes happens that many people together emerge simultaneously into Silver-Branch perception, into a Silver-Branch sense of being. It happened to the knights of the Round Table four hundred and fifty-four years after the passion and death and resurrection of Christ:

> And than the kynge and all the astatis wente home unto Camelot, and so wente unto evynsong to the grete monester. And so aftir upon that to sowper, and every knight sette in hys owne place as they were toforehonde.
>
> Than anone they harde crakynge and cryynge of thundir, that hem thought the palyse sholde all to-dryve. So in the myddys of the blast enfyrde a sonnebeame, more clerer by seven tymys than ever they saw day, and all were alighted of the grace of the Holy Goste. Than began every knight to beholde other, and eyther saw other, by their semynge, fayrer than ever they were before. Natforthan there was no knight that might speke one worde a grete whyle, and so they loked every man on other as they had bene doome.

Than entird into the halle the Holy Grayle covered with whyght samyte, but there was none that might se hit nother whom that bare hit. And there was all the halle fulfilled with good odours, and every knight had such metis and drynkes as he beste loved in thys worlde.

And whan the Holy Grayle had bene borne thorow the hall, than the holy vessel departed suddenly, that they wyst nat where hit becam. Than had they all breth to speke, and than the kyng yelded thankynges to God of Hys good grace that He had sente them.

Pentecost Sunday though it was, the Grail today and for now was covered in white samite and so, seeking a more open vision of it, these knights on the morrow rode through the street of Camelot and soon they had entered the dark wood of the world, a wood of paths more perplexed and perplexing than any of them, ever, even in dreams, had to take on. Here be witcheries. Here be sorceries suave and savage. Here be enchantments.

Here, treacherously, nothing is what it seems. Here, showing himself to be the fairest of maidens, is the great red dragon whose scream, when he does scream, quenches all fires in all realms near and far. Here be Nightmare and her Ninefold. Here, lying across your path, and looking ordinary, is a piece of deadwood that Nightmare herself, for fear of losing her already mad mind, wouldn't step over. Here, in this dark wood, it wouldn't be wise to rely on a pentangle of virtues blazoned on banner, shield and coat, or, as they would be spelled in adventurous times past, on banere, shelde and cote. The knyghtes of the Table Rounde have entered the heart of darkness. On a later adventure, it was with good reason that Sir Gawain prayed,

<blockquote>Cros Kryst me spede</blockquote>

Along some of its reaches the spiritual quest is an anious vyage.

Virtues we heraldically paraded at tourneys and parleys we won't parade now. Alone and without such prestige in the dark wood we find out what we are made of.

Walpurgis Nacht is the shadow side of Whit Sunday.

Whytsonday at Camelot. First there was a crakynge and a cryynge of thundir. And how greatly would we mistake this were we to think of it as meteorological thunder. This is the Grail Realm announcing itself. Next, seven times clearer than the light of day, the light and grace of the Holy Ghost enters the hall and settles on the seated knights, transfiguring them and rendering them speechless. Finally, filling the hall with heavenly fragrances, the Holy Grail enters. Mercifully, it is preciously covered, for who otherwise could endure the radiance. A blessed vessel, it moves around the Round Table and, under the species of whatever meat and drink each knight best likes, it distributes heavenly sustenance.

Objectively, that is what happened in Camelot on Whit Sunday. Subjectively, we can think of it as the coming of paradisal perception, because the Grail isn't only a thing, it is a way of perceiving no matter what thing, a shoe or a star. And that means that the knights didn't have to ride out in quest of it. It is as available right there in Camelot as it is elsewhere. It is as available to Yeats in a tea shop in London as it is to Edwin Muir, rustically roofed, in the Orkneys. Everything the knights saw Jacob Boehme saw, in a pewter dish.

> Ephphatha
> Be opened

Be opened and behold
Think of the apocalyptic 'Behold':

Behold, a great wonder in heaven, a woman clothed in the sun, with the Moon under her feet, and on her head a crown of twelve stars.

Healed of the anaesthetic built into our senses, all beholding, all perceiving and knowing, is apocalyptic. Wherever we happen to be, we look at an old boot, and we know that's it,

> Paradisal perception is ours
>
> The Grail Quest is accomplished.

Without a corresponding morality it will all have been in vain.
(*Slí Na Fírinne,* pp. 60–6)

Structured around three periods of chanted prayer and silent meditation:

7 – 8 am
12.30 – 1 pm
6 – 7 pm

On Saturday nights, from midnight, Tenebrae will be performed.

On Sunday mornings we will perform Ephphatha.

Believing that nature is revelation not veil we will spend time sacramentally alone in its great solitudes.

Whether inside or outside, work will be as little industrialized as possible.

Big engine sounds will be as rarely heard as possible.

Wherever possible, primitive tools not power tools.

Blackbird's eggs haven't had the time to adapt to modern mechanical noise, haven't had the time to soundproof themselves against the revving roars and the roaring drone of a chainsaw.

Ours is a house in a wood.

A wood you might meet Merlin in.

A wood Bran Mac Feabhail might have retired to.

Meet Bran in our wood and he will tell you that in every branch is the music of the Silver Branch.

The ethos of our house is in its hallows. They are:

> The Karmic Digging Fork
> The Tenebrae Harrow
> The Silver Branch

As we practise it, the adventure of our immortality includes and is kind to the adventure of our mortality.

It is our belief that Jesus has claimed the whole psyche for sanctity.

Nothing of what we are will be left behind on the purgatorial dancing floor. Our monastic day reflects and expresses our beliefs.

(*Slí Na Fírinne,* p. 154)

Hamlet to My Own Skull
— *On the Death Adventure* —

HAWK DREAMER
TIAMAT DREAMER
LEVIATHAN DREAMER
MOBY DICK DREAMER

And in the midst of life we are in death. Towards the end of his last book, John becomes aware that he is dying. And rather than live till he dies, he seems aware that dying itself is of the most sacred import. That we don't walk backwards into it. Can he have enough courage, enough observational nerve, enough hawk in him, that he can be 'Hamlet to my own skull'? Even as he encourages us to remove the word 'terminal' from his diagnosis – because something lives on – he acknowledges the passage he is consciously engaged in, the skeleton that has turned up at the door. It's terror of death that drives Gilgamesh, and it's final acceptance of death that marks him as a hero, far more than muscle and wit. As Moriarty turns his life, his thinking, his everything utterly over to his god, we behold a man drawing on all his song lines, night sea journeys, walks to the stable, nights in Gethsemane, to leave this dimension of time as a 'singing Christian'.

And I think something deepens in us when we witness our guide walk us to the door of the final, greatest mystery and sing his way through it. Very few writers in our time have so diligently sowed barley for coming generations like John has. Very few teachers in our time have led us to the watering hole or placed the four-pronged fork in our hand like John has. Very few humans have secreted our own, secret names in their prayers and turned such a naming into books, that Bright Angel Trail. There is a Christianity bigger than how we may as yet understand that word, and John loyally and ferociously responds to the awakening his Jesus bestows on him.

This last section is less a crow road for John Moriarty and more a hawk path as, having moved from the love adventure to the death adventure many years before, he shows what all real elders show us. Something about the business of dying. Dying not as identical to living but a Tenebrae all of itself, a ritual of not losing affection for the thrush, badger and Milky Way, but an opening to the great green fuse that threads through it all, the wonderful, exacting beholding of the music of what is.

John reminds us that the Irish for being buried is ta sid curtha, *'they are planted', and rather than laying the dead to rest they have* ta sid imithe ar Shli na Fírinne, *'set out on the Trail of Truth'.*

Over to you, God.

Up until the early decades of the last century, the peasants and villagers of Europe didn't wait passively for summer to come in. They brought it in, ceremonially. The following would be typical of what they did: the girls and boys would make a puppet of straw or of rags, calling it death. Carrying it out to throw it beyond the boundaries they would sing: 'We carry death out of the village.'

In some districts, they wouldn't just throw it intact across the boundary, nor would they be content to just throw it into a river asking the river to carry it out of their world: mocking it, jeering at it, they would tear death asunder and, setting fire to it, they would dance boisterously, still mocking, still jeering, about the flames. This done, the youngsters would then go into a wood, they would cut down a green bough or a young green tree, and, adorning it, they would carry it into the village singing a song traditional in their district, for example:

We have carried death out;
We are bringing the dear Summer back:
The Summer and the May
And all the flowers gay.

A charming custom. Not only charming, however. To someone who, with the Stoics, believes in the sympathy of all things, it is, also, a profoundly reasonable, even a profoundly inevitable, custom.

And yet I have difficulty with it. Bluntly: I am not sure that it is good practice to carry death out of our village.

I can of course see why we would want to carry out a negative understanding of death and throw it into a river that will carry it down into the swallowing, all-dissolving ocean. Having done this, though, it will then behove us to bring a new understanding of death, opening our doors to it now as an essential leaven of intensest, mortal life.

There is, Macbeth. There is something serious in mortality. It is serious even when it is forgotten during Suso's noon of heavenly lightnings, during Pascal's night of fire.

We carry death out of our village. Yes, we carry out all cosmologies that hurt the scars, all cosmologies that deaden and make dead the intensely living, intensely intelligent stars. We carry out Big Bang.

We carry out winter. Yes, we carry out our Gorgon-Cartesian, our petrifying perceptions of things. We carry out all thinking of and from the limits of contraction and opacity.

And we bring in Summer. Culturally we must bring it in.

As Leonardo, putting the finishing touch to the chiaroscuro of Mona's mouth, is bringing it in.

As the monk who walks mountains searching for the herbs from which he will make the inks and dyes for the Book of Kells is bringing it in.

As the young woman who, in a pub in Galway, picks up her fiddle and plays a familiar tune on it is bringing it in. Her rich, black hair tumbling down into the Mason's Apron, as if to listen, is bringing it in.

A man who lives in, but isn't entirely of, the modern world is walking to work one January morning. He looks across the bay, and the bogs, to where the Sun is coming over the horizon. He turns towards it and, raising his hands, as the green baboons of the Egyptian Book of the Dead do, he adores it. And he calls it by the name by which Nefertiti, standing in her mortuary chapel doorway, would have called it. He calls it Horakhty. Here on this wet, western road on a January morning, he speaks the brightest, divine name of the Brightest, Divine Being that ancient Egyptians had experience of Destitute himself, he speaks the greatest word of an ancient religion. And, looking across the bay and the bogs to Horakhty, he cannot now see in our great word or formula the meaning Einstein intended for it. Illuminated by Horakhty, E means ecstasy, m means Moksha and c is a hieroglyph for the uraeus-ringed retina of Einstein's third eye.

> *Now carry we Death out of the village*
> *And the new Summer into the village.*
> *Welcome, dear Summer,*
> *Sweet little corn.*

Now carry we 'single vision and Newton's sleep' out of our village. Cogito consciousness carry we out. Commonage consciousness carry we in.

> *Sumer is ycumen in*
> *Lude sing, cuccu!*
> *Groweth seed and bloweth med*
> *And springeth the wode nu.*
> *Sing, cuccu!*
> *Awe bleeteth after lamb*
> *Lowth after calve cu*

HAMLET TO MY OWN SKULL

Bulloc sterteth, bucke verteth
Merie sing, cuccu!
Cuccu, cuccu.
Wel singes thu, cuccu;
Ne swink thu never nu!

Singing it, we bring the Mandukya Om into our village. Speaking them outside every door of our village, we bring new words into our village. Knowing new possibilities of summer understanding, of summer growing, in them, we sing them: Nirguna Brahman, Saguna Brahman, Shabda Brahman, Anantashaya, Shakti, Mayashakti, Kundalashakri, chakra, Bhakti yoga, Jnana yoga, Jivanmukta, Mahavakya, Mandukya Om.

Wel singes thu, cuccu;

And where do you come from? asks the young woman sitting beside me in the bus. From a place inside me I say. From a farm inside me. From a farm far away inside me called Fern Hill I say.

Your name, please? the man in the passport office asked me.

Honoured among wagons, I replied. That's my name on Monday. On Tuesday the blackbirds call me Prince of the apple towns. On Wednesday the geese call me Famous among the barns. On Thursday the owls who are carrying me away call me Nightly under the simple stars. On Friday morning coming home I am The Wanderer white with the dew, the cock on my shoulder. On Saturday alone on the hills I am The Farm forever fled. On Sunday, there it is, summer again, Fern Hill again, horses again, the spellbound horses walking warm out of the whinnying green stables on to the fields of praise.

Horses walking spellbound, constellations walking spellbound. Ursa, Aries, Capricorn, Cancer, Leo, Virgo walking spellbound, Taurus walking spellbound on to the fields of praise.

Dylan came singing summer. He came bringing a new first page for our Holy Book.

Like horses, we have all walked spellbound out of a whinnying green stable on to the fields of praise.

Wel singes thu, cuccu,
Ne swink thu never nu!

Words we bring: viksepa shakti, avarana shakti, adhyaropa.

Words from where words fall away: avarana, Klesa avarana, Jneya avarana, ashraya paravritti, padmasambhava, ratnasambhava, vajrayana, vajrasattva, prajna paramita.

Earth we call it. Tellurically, Earth. Chthonically, Earth. For us who live on it, it is or it should be Big Medicine. And looking at it from a distance, looking at it from the Moon, it wouldn't be amiss to think of it as padmasambhava, Ratnasambhava. Looking at it from a wet, western road on a January morning walking to work, it wouldn't be amiss to call it Buddh Gaia.

From Once-Upon-a-Time we are, we sing, coming home to our village.

From a farm far away within we are, we sing.

From Buddh Gaia we are, we sing, the cocks whose crowing will awaken us awake on our shoulders.

And we are glad, because we who walked spellbound, walk wide awake now, in the fields of praise.

Ne swink ye never nu! Cucuricu, Cucuricu,
Crow ye nu
Cucuricu, Cucuricu, Cucuricu.

(*Dreamtime*, pp. 209–12)

Death, a Native American has said, is not an end, it is a change of worlds.

Death, I would say, is a change from one way of being in the Divine Mirum to another way of being in it.

Death isn't the worst thing that can happen to a person. Also, as Garry McMahon recently reminded me, we are so much bigger than the lives we live that we shouldn't be too upset about leaving them when our work here below is done.

In comparison with all of this of course, cancer and chemotherapy are direct prose. And yet, I think of them as the Eucharist of cancer and chemotherapy, that even though, in its side effects, some of the stuff that was drip-fed into me was straight up out of hell's kitchen.

Long drawn out sometimes, and wasting us, ghosting us, the diseases from which some of us die give death a bad name.

The thing to do is to separate death from disease.

It is of disease not of death that we should ask, Where now, after death has rescued us, is thy victory, where now thy sting?

In all of this I am, I believe, dealing in facts, not in trite consolations.

Can I be Hamlet to my own skull in the cemetery in Elsinore? Can I take it in my hands and think about it and talk about it in ways quite other than the way in which he talked about Yorick's skull? Can I not estimate it in a Buddhist way, seeing its emptiness positively, as without the avarannas or obscurations of passion and thought? Can I not estimate it as St John of the Cross has:

> O wretched condition of this life wherein it is so dangerous to live and so difficult to find the truth. That which is most clear and true is to us most obscure and doubtful and we therefore avoid it though it is most necessary for us. That which shines the most and dazzles our eyes, that we embrace and follow after though it is most hurtful to us and makes us stumble at every step. In what fear and danger then must man be living, seeing that the very light of his natural eyes by which he directs his steps is the very first to bewilder and deceive him when he would draw near unto God. If he wishes to be sure of the road he travels on he must close his eyes and walk in the dark if he is to journey in safety from his domestic foes which are his own senses and faculties.

My senses and faculties help me to find the way from here to Killarney but on the way back to God they bewilder and impede me.

A HUT AT THE EDGE OF THE VILLAGE

I think of a Hamlet who goes not to Wittenberg, to university there, but to Cologne, there to receive the highest of higher educations, from Meister Eckhart. That way we might hear something worthwhile from him in the cemetery in Elsinore. As it is, this cemetery is graveyard to something more than the people who are buried in it.

Has it come to this, Ophelia in her madness buried beneath the skull and crossbones, no, beneath the skull and haphazard bones of a jester, a joker?

The entire human drama, with its Alexanders and its Caesars, has it come to this, has it come to Hamlet's

Pah!

Hamlet: Dost thou think Alexander looked o' this fashion i' the Earth?
Horatio: E'en so.
Hamlet: And smelt so? pah!
Horatio: E'en so, my Lord.

It is probably how Beckett would rename a greatly reduced version of Shakespeare's play,

Pah!

Beckett and Dylan Thomas.
I think of Dylan in the cemetery in Elsinore. I think of him over-singing and out-singing the singing gravedigger:

And death shall have no dominion.
Dead men naked they shall be one
With the man in the wind and the west Moon;
When their bones are picked clean and the clean bones gone,
They shall have stars at elbow and foot;
Though they go mad they shall be sane;
Though they sink through the sea they shall rise again;

Though lovers be lost love shall not;
And death shall have no dominion.

Though she died mad, singing a mad song, Ophelia shall be sane. Though she lies beneath the bones of a joker, she shall have stars at elbow and foot. In her are depths unreachable to death's scythe. Death shall have no dominion over her. But neither, the Buddha would say, will risen, ego-centred, incarnate life have dominion over her. It isn't only a question, he would say, of shaking off the mortal coil. It is a question also of shaking off the sense of self and dualizing mind about which it is coiled:

> Through many rounds from birth
> To death have I toiled, seeking
> But not finding the builder of the house.
> House-builder, I behold you now,
> Again a house you will not build.
> All your rafters are broken now,
> The ridgepole also is destroyed.
> My mind, its elements dissolved,
> The end of craving has attained.

The Buddha looking more deeply ruinous, and ruined, than Christ on Calvary.

Not for him Dylan's nature mysticism. Not for him a final condition of being one with the man in the wind and the west Moon:

> A self and what pertains to the self are not to be found in truth and actuality.

Is it not time that our Upanishads, Christian and other, were our coffin texts.

I think of Hamlet buried in the Mandukya Upanishad.

I think of Ophelia buried in the Kena Upanishad.

I think of Yorick, the jester, buried in the Chandogya Upanishad.

That's it, the gravedigger changing his tune in the cemetery in Elsinore.

As for myself, I would like to see Eckhart's account of our final transition into God inscribed on the underside of my coffin lid:

> Comes then the soul into the unclouded light of God. It is transported so far from creaturehood into nothingness that, of its own powers, it can never return to its agents or its former creaturehood. Once there, God shelters the soul's nothingness with his uncreated essence, safeguarding its creaturely existence. The soul has dared to become nothing, and cannot pass from its own being into nothingness and then back again, losing its own identity in the process, except God safeguarded it. This must needs be so.

And, he too having died, in what Upanishad shall we bury the gravedigger? How about this:

> *En una noche oscura,*
> *Con ansias en amores inflamada,*
> *Oh dichosa ventura!*
> *Sali sin ser notada*
> *Estando ya mi casa sosegada …*

And what new song for the new gravedigger? How about this:

> *Oh noche, que guiaste,*
> *Oh noche amable mas que el alborada:*
> *Oh noche que juntaste*
> *Amado con amada,*
> *Amada en el Amado transformada!*

Come to think of it, this bhakta's Udana would better suit Ophelia, she, as I imagine her, singing much as Suso sang:

> When the good and faithful servant enters into the joy of his Lord, he is inebriated by the riches of the house of God; for he feels, in an ineffable degree, that which is felt by an inebriated man. He forgets himself, he is no longer conscious of his selfhood: he disappears and

loses himself in God, and becomes one spirit with Him, as a drop of water which is drowned in a great quantity of wine. For even as such a drop disappears, taking the colour and the taste of wine, so is it with those who are in full possession of blessedness …

She, as I imagine her, singing much as Marguerite Porete sang:

Being completely free, and in command of her sea of peace, the soul is nonetheless drowned and loses herself through God, with him and in him. She loses her identity, as does the water from a river – like the Ouse or the Meuse – when it flows into the sea. It has done its work and can relax in the arms of the sea, and the same is true of the soul. Her work is over and she can lose herself in what she has totally become: Love – Love is the bridegroom of her happiness enveloping her wholly in his love and making her part of that which is. This is a wonder to her and she has become a wonder …

And, as Marguerite will tell us, this isn't yet the end.

It is time to let Eckhart throw a lifeline to Shakespeare. More generally, it is time to let mysticism throw a lifeline to literature. Mostly, literature continues to flourish where Plato would expect to find it, in the cave.

Let Eckhart, not Beckett, have the final say in the cemetery in Elsinore:

Oh, wonder of wonders, when I think of the union the soul has with God! He makes the enraptured soul to flee out of herself, for she is no more satisfied with anything that can be named. The spring of Divine Love flows out of the soul and draws her out of herself into the unnamed Being, into her first source, which is God alone.

> Our bhakta's Udana.
> Our destined Udana.
> Our God-willed Udana.

The enraptured Udana of sandgrain and star.

So yes, nature in me had turned against itself but, not without reason, I did sometimes think that this wasn't the whole story. The hawk I had shaken hands with in an earlier dream, or should I say the hawk I had shaken hands and legs with, or, going yet further back in evolutionary time, the hawk I had shaken fins with, now again he showed up in a dream that I sensed was his more than mine. As some dreams go, it was short but hugely sure of itself. I am sitting in my chair by the fire, writing. Eileen is sitting at the other side, reading. Aware of him to begin with in peripheral vision, I look through the window and I see him diving fiercely down among a scatter of small birds, they taking off, alive but alarmed, in desperate, frightened flight. The next thing I see is that he is just beyond my window, tilted unhoveringly there, showing his wide-winged back to me. I draw Eileen's attention to him. Looking at him for what seems forever, we are both utterly charmed and, belonging for now in a world alternatively perceived and known, our whole house itself is utterly charmed.

The question was, how to inherit and inhabit this dream? In the sense in which a Native American would understand the idea, am I a hawk dreamer and if so what is expected of me? Must I dress like the Palaeolithic birdman and live ecumenically towards all things? Must I be symphonic with all things? Must I go yet farther, must I be homeophonic with all things? Must I bell with the stag, call with the eagle, grunt with the boar, sing with the lark? Must I come back down from our evolutionary height, if height it is, and be natural in the way that all natural things are natural? Must I deliver myself up to nature in the way that Wordsworth delivered up Lucy Gray to it? Wouldn't that mean being a predator with a good con- science? Wouldn't that mean being murderous with a good conscience? Wouldn't it mean being a flesh-eater, shearing muscle off a gazelle's bones, with a good conscience? Wouldn't this be an abdication of moral responsibility and, however evanescent it might be, isn't moral responsibility a chief evolutionary wonder of our astronomical surroundings? Isn't it the pride and prestige of the galaxy in which it shows up? Isn't it the pride and prestige of the black hole that might pull it down into extinction? What compared to it is the explosive enormity of a supernova? What compared to it is the fragrance of a primrose? Could it be that the moral life lived in accordance with moral principles requires separation from nature?

I think of two Dreamtime fights for the Irish soul. One is the fight between Balar and Manannán. It is a fight for pre-eminence in us between Súil Mildagach perception and Silver-Branch perception. The other is a good-hearted fight or struggle between Oisín the pagan and St Patrick the Christian. At its starkest, Oisín invites us to listen to the blackbird, invites us in other words to seek fulfilment in immanence whereas, with his Christian bell, St Patrick invites us to seek final fulfilment in transcendence.

I look at African hunting dogs snapping at a hyena and I think, to seek for salvation in nature is to seek for it in what itself needs salvation. So why should I capitulate, sinking all the way back down from moral responsibility to snapping, eye-toothed consciencelessness? Or have I got it all wrong? Can I not become a hawk dreamer without any such capitulation, without any such abdication? In living from a depth within myself where 'I' is 'we', am I not already a hawk dreamer, a pteranodon dreamer, an ammonite dreamer? Is it not sufficient that my central nervous system has become a sympathetic nervous system? Is it not sufficient that I live sympathetically with everything inside me and around me? With my reptile brain and with the rattlesnake challenging me to keep my distance?

Essential to sanctity, whether in the Palaeolithic or in our day, is a willingness to live ecumenically with all things – more essential to it is a willingness to live sympathetically with all things.

So yes, as a Christian, and without moral capitulation, I can be a hawk dreamer. I can say:

> In drinking from the karmic cup, Jesus instituted we-awareness at the origin and heart of Christianity and, to that extent at least, thunder dreamers and Tiamat dreamers and hawk dreamers should

feel at home in it. It is Christianity as it should have been from the beginning that we are talking about. I think of Black Elk evangelizing the four Evangelists, Matthew, Mark, Luke and John.

And so, empowered by Christ, I say it:

Help me, Hawk.

Help me to build a Christian monastic hedge school called Slí na Fírinne. Much as the animals of his locality helped Ciarán of Saighir in a similar venture, help me in this, a first small attempt to bring in and ground the new Christian epoch.

Counterculturally to Marduk, I will brave it, saying:

Hawk dreamer I am.
Tiamat dreamer I am.
Leviathan dreamer I am.
Moby-Dick dreamer I am.

And I think of our Evangelists, Matthew saying, Eagle dreamer I am; Mark saying, Ox dreamer I am; Luke saying, Lion dreamer I am; and John saying, Deinanthropus dreamer I am.

I think of Black Elk. It is in acknowledging and recognizing him as a Pleistocene thunder dreamer of our day that I would welcome him into Christianity.

Thunder dreamers we need.

Leviathan dreamers we need.

Dragon dreamers, not dragon slayers, we need.

Tsetsekia we need, not a bull-bellowing, echoing Labyrinth under our cities and, therefore, under our psyches.

And so, it delights me beyond measure to see rosary beads in a thunder- dreamer's hands.

A Blackfoot girl called Gets Up Off Her Tepee Floor and a Lakota boy called Black Elk: compared to their world-saving deeds, what here in Europe can we expect from such imagined frailties as Lucy Gray and Emile?

It shows, even when we think we have been shaped by it, how cut off from nature we are. Especially does it show how cut off from the thaumaturgically self-healing universe we are.

We are spectators not participators. Not participators, certainly, in the way that Gets Up Off Her Tepee Floor and Black Elk are.

The truth is we are far more astronomically far-seeing on Blackfoot dancing ground than on Mount Palomar.

A thunder dreamer on Blackfoot dancing ground, him I would first consult about the life of the universe, only then an astronomer on Mount Palomar.

And here's a question: To what extent is our Hubble eye a Balar's eye? In it's means and mode, how unlike Manannán's *at-chíu* is it?

So there it is,

> the thaumaturgically self-healing universe,

our culture and our history telling us that, while it is out there all around us, it seemingly isn't in us, this perhaps a reason why we are the permanent perpetrators of a permanent Ragnarok. Or is it that we are Ragnarok, irrespective of whether we are hawk dreamers or not? It was in a time when we were auroch dreamers, mammoth dreamers, lion dreamers, woolly rhinoceros dreamers that we speared the bison bull, that we speared nature in its power to generate, this the dolorous stroke that replaced we-awareness with us-and-them awareness, this the dolorous stroke that turned Merlin into Bacon, that turned Logrys into John Locke Land.

Ascribing the name backwards in time into the Palaeolithic, I think of our European Serengeti. I think of it at its most various and most prosperous. Then I think of it decimated. And the little that remained, that in turn decimated. And, fearing neither a lion leap from behind him nor a rhinoceros charge from in front of him, there he is now, Cézanne out of doors, seeking to restore its radiance to Mont Sainte-Victoire.

What are we without the rhinoceros charge in our midst? What are we without the lion leap in our midst? What are we as the lords and masters of the little that's left? I had imagined my father having a Native American name, Man Walking Behind Cows. Should I risk such a name, calling myself Shakes Hands With Hawk? Or, turning the thing inwards, should I call myself, Shakes Hands With The Fin In His Hand? It was holding a pen in a hand that has evolved from a fin that Dante wrote the *Paradiso*, that Blake wrote 'Auguries of Innocence', that Benjamin Franklin drafted some of the articles of the American constitution.

Cézanne in our herdless Serengeti. Before anything else, Paul, paint the hand that paints. Paint the hand that launched the lance into the bison bull's genitals. Being the Master of Animals, that bull is in a sense all animals. And the Fisher King who has reproductively inherited the lance, he in a sense is all human males. And so it is that Sir Gawain setting out to heal the Fisher King is Sir Gawain setting out to heal himself also.

I would think of a dream. Walking between Male and Female, between Marie Hughes and Leon Moscona, a sword that had been a long time lodged in it fell out of my phallus. Short though it was, it seemed like an epochal dream, and it left me with questions I scarcely dared to ask: did the Palaeolithic dolorous stroke and its consequences come to an end in me right there by the upper lake in Glendalough? And Marie Hughes, she, the Woman, did she, by her intervention, help to bring the whole thing to a blessed conclusion?

Maybe so. And if so, then our return to we-awareness, then full cultural encouragement and approval for dreamers, for thunder dreamers, for hawk dreamers.

I could see them now, some of the events that defined my life, giving it shape and direction: in adult understanding and inheritance my baptismal assimilation to Christ crossing the Torrent; Ragnarok inner and outer under a mountain in the Inagh Valley; the Karmic Digging Fork turning up in my hand; the sword falling out of my phallus; my handshake with the hawk.

Looking back on it now, it seemed like a progress I had no choice in, a destiny. Like it or not, a countercultural drama would enact itself in me. Once I went down into it, the Grand Canyon became my permanent, real address. And once I caught sight of the Earth coming up over its own karmic horizon, once I caught sight of Buddh Gaia, there was no turning away, no not serving the vision. And once I discovered that in the unfallen core of my soul I am the Kedushah, how could I not let it sing itself all the way out through all that I am, good and bad? And knowing that it has happened to so many before me, how can I not at all times live in the imminence of final eureka or, as Muslim mystics more justly know it, of fana and baqa?

Myth-sized destiny that it was, there was no resisting it or elegant ordering of it. In living it or in writing about it, a will to elegance would betray it.

There was anguish and suffering in all of this. Fisher King anguish and suffering. The suffering and anguish of phylogenetic self-encounter, Idumea and Nebuchadnezzar ever in the offing. The anguish and suffering of deinanthropic self-experience, of knowing myself no-man-fathomed. The anguish and suffering of seeking to stay awake with Christ in the Canyon.

One night I was carried down into what I thought must be the darkest and deepest and most forgotten pit of hell and down there I thought, this invalidates the universe, every shining star of it. And while I prayed from that depth as I held on to the cruciform root of a sycamore tree I was carried yet farther down into a lostness that, if it looked down into it, would bring a cold sweat out through deepest hell and down there I thought, this invalidates God. And yet, this was not a failure of faith. If anything it deepened it. During the not-so-small hours I came round to thinking that maybe I myself was the one who must undergo invalidation. Invalidation before God in the course of being redeemed by God. And was this Good Friday from the sixth to the ninth hour – abandonment by God and invalidation before God? But I was and I still am on shaky ground here, so back to the hawk.

A HUT AT THE EDGE OF THE VILLAGE

In Dublin for chemo, I travelled down with Neill McCann to his house in the Glen of the Downs in County Wicklow. We went out to walk in the wood. As soon as we entered it, a kestrel called above us. Accompanying us all the way, turning when we turned, he called, called, called, not threateningly, not in instinctive reaction, but as though he wished to fall in with us, making us three, our apparent difference in species not a difference in deep, essential kind.

A few days later, back in Kerry, Eileen and myself travelled to Tubrid Well, a Marian shrine, near Millstreet in County Cork. Local lore has it that if you see a fish in the visibly springing, sparkling pool, you will be healed. We didn't see a fish but on the way home a kestrel dropped down on to a telephone cable that crossed the road just ahead of us and there was something in the way that he looked down not so much at us as into us. Something not explainable in terms of current assumptions about things.

The one thing I was sure of in all this is that I in particular was not the issue. So what in fact is the issue? As I see it, it is a choice we must make between shaking hands with the hawk and splicing hands with Ahab. To splice hands with Ahab in the murderous destruction of Moby-Dick is to splice hands with Marduk in the murderous destruction of Tiamat, it is to splice hands with Atum in the murderous destruction of Apophis, it is to splice hands with Baal in the murderous destruction of Yam, it is to splice hands with Yahweh in the murderous destruction of Leviathan, it is to splice hands with Zeus in the murderous destruction of Typhon, it is to splice hands with St George and later on with Siegfried in the murderous destruction of the Dragon, it is to splice hands with the ancient or not-so-ancient Mariner in the destruction of the Albatross, he the bird who made the favouring breeze to blow. It isn't only the Albatross who hangs from our necks, Tiamat, Apophis, Yam, Leviathan, Typhon and the Dragon hang from them also.

(*Curlew,* pp. 337–45)

Here in Kerry, on a silent night after rain, I go out and listen to the monotonal roar of high corrie lakes rushing down through the Cummar and I know what the Mandukya Upanishad knows, that the universe that surrounds and inhabits me is Brahmanirguna in astronomical self-manifestation.

Looking some days at it, I know that Torc Mountain is the Divine Mirum in theophany to itself within itself.

In my early twenties I crossed into the love adventure and in my early fifties I crossed into the death adventure and, all in all I suppose, I emerged as enriched from the one as I already know I will from the other.

As well as graduating from anthropus into deinanthropus in Connemara I graduated into Silver-Branch perception there and so it is that I see things as mirabilia and so it is in turn that I so often experience myself as Miranda in nature and name.

I have for a long time practised the ritual of closing my eyes and mind to the world in Tenebrae and opening my eyes and mind to the world in Ephphatha.

I believe that experience of Silver-Branch perception and of Silver-Branch ontology must give rise to Silver-Branch morality.

Late in the day all beastliness in me showed itself docile to sanctification and this justifies what our little sister is doing, she leading the repressed back among us.

As though nature itself would inaugurate a Birdreign, I shook hands, at his hovering invitation, with a hawk.

Every time I tell their stories, I am Narada and A'noshma: as Narada I walk into inner and outer Ragnarok with Vishnu, as A'noshma I dive to the floor of the abyss in search of the seed sound out of which a world might emerge. It was in that Maidu quest that I heard the self-singing Song of Origins that the Maori heard a long, long time ago, and that I came back with.

A HUT AT THE EDGE OF THE VILLAGE

Every time I tell Sir Gawain's story, I ride north to the chaunce of the chapel.

In a final retelling, Sir Gawain does accept Sir Bertilak's invitation to ride back to his castle with him. True to his word, he introduces the now not-so-knightly knight to Morgan le Faye. Scarlet with little white tufts on it, and telling him as she does so that it is the meaning of his adventure, she places an amanita muscaria cap on his head. Seeing him to the door, she says, As you ride south through it, educate England.

As for myself, having Cú Roí mac Dáire in mind, having how he founded Irish philosophy in mind, it is, I imagine, with my father's quenched lantern that I walk south through the land.

Our quenched dualizing mind, our quenched lantern: I think of it as a mahavakya:

Yatra na anyat pasyati, na anyat srinoti, na anyat vijanati, sa bhuma.

Where nothing else is seen, nothing else is heard, nothing else is thought about, there is the Divine Plenitude.

Now when I go down into my own unconscious I do not stop short where Greek myth and where Freud did, at the end of Ariadne's thread, facing all that I phylogenetically am. Hearing a supernal music, I continue downwards, down, down, down until, back at home in it, I become the singing I ontologically am at the core of my soul.

At the core of my soul,

> The Kedushah I am.
> The Trishagion I am.
> The Sanctus I am.

> The everlasting hymn of praise to God I am.

Holy, holy, holy, Lord God of hosts, heaven and Earth are full of your glory.

Sanctus, sanctus, sanctus, Dominus Deus Sabaoth, pleni sunt caeli et terra gloria tua.

Welcoming this self-singing Sanctus all the way outwards into all that I am, good and bad, is my Eucharist from within. It is therapy not often thought of or practised.

Being a mantra it can go on for a long, long time:

The self-singing Sanctus that I am at the core of my soul, I welcome it all the way outwards through all that I am good and bad.

The self-singing Sanctus that I am at the core of my soul, I welcome it all the way outwards through all that I am good and bad.

The self-singing Sanctus that I am at the core of my soul, I welcome it all the way outwards through all that I am good and bad.

On another day, in another mood, this is what comes to the fore:

In the unfallen core of my soul I am myself the Paradise I walk in.

In the unfallen core of my soul I am myself the Paradise I walk in.

In the unfallen core of my soul I am myself the Paradise I walk in.

All that, and more.
More by way of mantra practice.
More by way of waiting in self-abeyance upon God.
And this too turns to mantra:

I rejoice in the God I can have no empirical experience of.

I rejoice in the God I can have no empirical experience of.

I rejoice in the God I can have no empirical experience of.

Here now, forever, I rejoicingly let go of my needs for an empirical experience of God.
Here now, forever, I rejoicingly let go of my needs for an empirical experience of God.
Here now, forever, I rejoicingly let go of my needs for an empirical experience of God.

I go for broke, leaving all that I naturally and supernaturally am, leaving all I in any way am, behind me in trackless dark Infinity.

Over to you, God.

In the meantime, Nostos.

'It is a small step for me,' he said.
'It is a small step for me but a giant step for humanity.'
Altogether more significant is a journey to

The Earth.

Altogether more significant than our journey to being

Man on the Moon

is our journey to being

Buddh Gaians

on

Buddh Gaia.

(*Curlew*, pp. 374–6)

Genius in Every Stone

— *On Sore Amazement* —

And here we are. We shuffled into the hut at the dusk, and now it's dawn, maybe a dawn many weeks after our arrival. We got smoked over, chanted over, pickled, spun around, dissolved and remade. Sometimes there was no longer the fire and hut, but savannah, northern forests and a Grail castle, a starving Irish philosopher hitching his way home for Christmas.

We saw hugeness in there, didn't we?

We were flummoxed, moved and frustrated, all the good stuff. A Moriartian way is not a balm, a sedative, a Post-it note, a hashtag. It's too restless for that, he's too restless for that. There's some kind of vocational lonesomeness that, while not perpetually anguished, has an uncivilized longing in it. It doesn't fit. You can't really franchise Celtic Christianity from the organization of his thoughts. He's too subtle for that. Too wild for that. He's at that seal hole now, talking quietly with Sylvia Plath and Leonard Crow Dog.

Moriarty is a high-stakes thinker, and he encourages us to not let ourselves off such a metaphysical hook either. But it could be just a fragment we choose to deepen into. What would it mean to learn just one of the old Irish Fianna tales to tell orally? What would it mean to track a hare and lie in its warm impression in the long grass? What would it mean to be known in your community as 'the singing lad' or the 'singing girl?' Not as an act of ventriloquism, but authenticity. Become a scholar of wonderful things, a student of beautiful learning.

In two decades of leading wilderness rites of passage, I've learned something. No matter how marvellous the mountain-top epiphany, no matter how deep the vigil in the forest, if you cannot craft a gift from the experience in the end the encounter will never quite accomplish itself. It may malfunction. It's a three-step programme, not a two-step one. Severance from the daily, encounter with the more than human, the return. And the return, in time, is always an act of gift-giving to the people. I would suggest we got our breath, our mind, our heart round the challenge of these writings. It's not something to be conquered, or sublimated, or reduced, but joyfully submitted to.

Let us not be selfish with John's work. There are rarely writers as initiatory in tone as he is, and if that's the register, the pitch, the incant, then it too follows the same three-step patterning. In some quite wonderful, quite tricksy way, what we learned in John's hut will only start to bless us when we start to communicate a little of it ourselves. It's always been like this. He did it himself with his honorary elders – all the myriad writers and poets with whom he endlessly dialogues. Those piles of books he had around him at home tell us something about community. And they tell us something about handling loneliness when you have a mind the size of a prairie.

His noble dead *are* his Round Table, his Inklings, his Eranos. Those tottering piles of books are nothing less than a Stonehenge in both their preservation and stimulation of our man. They are ritual, seanced devices. His seelie and unseelie court, his gabble of Temenos. Thank God for them. They are not just life-savers but life-makers.

The thoughts he loves are a community, a conversation, a dialogue it can be hard to find in your immediate locality. Moriarty is writing for the ear of Blake, Jacob Boehme, Crazy Horse, just as much as us. He is singing for the pleasure of curlew, bull and grizzly, just as much as us. You will know this by now. I wonder if his imaginative community saved him proper, unhelpful despair. We sit between Euripides and Captain Ahab – at peace at last – at a Greek tragedy of Moriarty's devising on the life and times of John the Baptist.

That's called singing the soul back home.

So, thank you, John.
For us adrift in Big Mike's boat,
I say thank you.
For us sleeping harsh on a London bench,
I say thank you.
For us troubled in the yard with no lantern lit,
I say thank you.

DR MARTIN SHAW is a storyteller who lives by a river in Dartmoor national park. An award-winning writer, mythologist and teacher, he is currently Reader in Poetics at Dartington Arts School. Shaw founded both the Oral Tradition and Mythic Life courses at Stanford University. His translations of Gaelic poetry and folklore (with Tony Hoagland) have been published in *Orion Magazine, Poetry International, Kenyon Review, Poetry Magazine* and *The Mississippi Review*. Shaw's most recent books include *The Night Wages, Wolferland, All Those Barbarians, Courting the Wild Twin* and his Lorca translations, *Courting the Dawn* (with Stephan Harding). His essay and conversation with Ai Weiwei on myth and migration was released by the Marciano Arts foundation. For twenty years he has been a wilderness rites-of-passage guide, and lived for four years in a black tent on a succession of English hills.

For more on Martin Shaw's work:
cistamystica.com | schoolofmyth.com | drmartinshaw.com

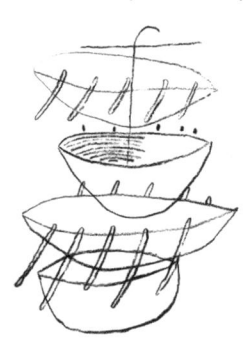